The Woman in Apartment 2

A Story of Love, Loss, and Learning to Let Go

The Woman in Apartment 2

A Story of Love, Loss, and Learning to Let Go

Paul M. Spinella

Published by Game Changer Publishing

Paperback ISBN: 978-1-963793-81-9
Hardcover ISBN: 978-1-963793-82-6
Digital: ISBN: 978-1-963793-83-3

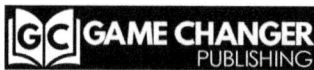

GC GAME CHANGER PUBLISHING

www.GameChangerPublishing.com

DEDICATION

This book is dedicated to God, the Universe, my friends, and my family. Most importantly, to the woman in Apartment 2, thank you for shining light on all my pieces, reminding me of what boundaries are, and embracing differences. Thank you for your love, laughter, and joy, and for choosing to share your couch with me.

The Woman in Apartment 2

A Story of Love, Loss, and Learning to Let Go

Paul M. Spinella

GC GAME CHANGER PUBLISHING

www.GameChangerPublishing.com

"Grief, I've learned, is really just love. It's all the love you want to give, but cannot. All that unspent love gathers up in the corners of your eyes, the lump in your throat, and in that hollow part of your chest. Grief is just love with no place to go."

– Jamie Anderson

Foreword

One immutable truth about Paul is that he is one of those "all-or-nothing" guys. When he does something—anything—he throws himself into it with the force of a tsunami, or he doesn't do it at all.

So when Paul asked me to read the manuscript for this book, I was sure he would thoroughly immerse himself in it. He would cut no corners. He would not shortchange the reader by producing a surface-level story; instead, he would create a work that contained not just his heart and soul but several other vital organs.

My assessment was accurate. *The Woman in Apartment 2* is not merely a work about Paul's relationship with a woman and the joys and sorrows that accompany it. Certainly, it is that. But it is also a candid, soul-baring exploration into Paul's psyche, a testament to his commitment to self-understanding and truth.

The Woman in Apartment 2 highlights the experiences of his upbringing and early adult life that gave him the internal fortitude to handle adversity. At the same time, it describes how many of those events broke him down emotionally and psychologically, making him question his inherent worth and whether he deserved a long-term relationship in which his partner would love him just the way he is, scars and all.

True to his disdain for halfway approaches, Paul delves into a level of welcoming and shocking detail. He pulls no punches in describing the highs and lows of his relationship—the strong connection he would feel with the woman in Apartment 2 when they engaged in the simplest activities and the mind-numbing realization that some fundamental differences between them might make a genuine, long-term connection impossible.

Primarily, *The Woman in Apartment 2* describes how a giving, loving, but emotionally fragile man, with the aid and support of a tenacious yet sensitive therapist, was able to turn a serious relationship into a catalyst for personal transformation and growth. Learning that his imperfections didn't make him inferior; they just made him human. Regaining a sense of self-worth and truly believing that he deserves all the good things that come his way. Most importantly—as trite as it may sound—realizing that love for oneself must firmly be in place before it can be given to anyone else.

Each one of us has or will endure the loss of a relationship we were convinced would last a lifetime. Such a loss can trigger and elicit similar feelings and doubts for our own emotional and moral makeup. Traveling alongside Paul during his highly charged emotional journey may give you the impetus to ask yourself the same questions Paul asked of himself and come away, like Paul, with a deeper understanding and appreciation of who you are. This journey, while challenging, holds the potential for profound personal growth and self-discovery.

I wouldn't call *The Woman in Apartment 2* a self-help book, but it may be just that for some of you. That's, of course, assuming you throw yourself into it with the same "all-or-nothing" attitude that Paul did when he wrote it.

– Art Sesnovich, Principal, Bulldog Communications

Table of Contents

Introduction

*T*he *Woman in Apartment 2* is more than a book; it's a courageous narrative of love, loss, and the art of letting go. It's a brave recounting of the obstacles that once held me captive, transformed through the discovery of a different kind of love, acceptance, forgiveness, and a deepened connection with God, my children, and, ultimately, myself. This narrative stands as a testament to the resilience of the human spirit and the transformative power of embracing one's own truth.

In the spring of 2021, I experienced the end of a relationship that left me emotionally paralyzed. Though no stranger to heartache and loss, this particular experience cut deeper than any before, leaving me to question my own worthiness and lovability. In the pursuit of healing, I found myself at a crossroads, compelled to question everything.

Delving into the metaphorical boxes of abuse, neglect, and trauma that I had carried for 38 years became an essential part of my healing process. Seated uncomfortably on my therapist's couch with a cup of coffee in hand, I bravely unpacked each and every box. The lessons learned during this pivotal period were indispensable to my healing journey. These lessons, while uniquely mine, underscore a universal truth—that we are all capable of healing and inherently deserving of love when we confront ourselves with honesty.

There are seasons in life when we feel shattered beyond repair. Our moments of brokenness often shape our perception of worthiness, and the scars of abandonment, abuse, and heartbreak can convince us that we are undeserving of love—the very essence from which God created us to be. The scars left by abandonment, abuse, and heartbreak can insidiously convince us that we are unworthy of the love we were inherently created to receive.

As you embark on the chapters of this book, my fervent hope is that it serves as a poignant reminder—a whisper that resonates in your soul—that you are undeniably worthy and deserving to be seen. May it affirm, with unwavering certainty, that you are loved beyond measure.

CHAPTER 1

Dive Bars

I should have been over the moon. I should have been celebrating a six-month anniversary with a woman I had grown to love and cherish deeply. Instead, I found myself hanging onto a text I had received from her earlier that day, a text that read, *"I really need to talk to you about something."* I was 37 years old and had just dug my way out of some significant life events—events that had shaped and molded me into the very person who was now sitting alone at a Midwest dive bar across the street from my girlfriend's apartment complex.

She had asked me to arrive at her apartment at 7:30 p.m., and I was early. We both had a habit of arriving 15 minutes late to any event (we were similar in many respects), but I wanted to be on time for this one. I had been ruminating since I received her text and found myself lost in a blunder of racing thoughts. I felt certain I knew what this talk meant and that certainty had me stuck in my head, consumed by thoughts of an impending breakup that I was neither ready nor willing to accept. When I could no longer stand the tension, I drove to her apartment—two hours and thirty minutes earlier than we'd arranged.

I wanted to believe I was wrong and thought my fear would dissipate when I showed up to her apartment and saw her front door. That door was a gateway to a place that had felt like home from the very first moment I ever walked in. It was an old apartment door connected to a short, uneven walkway caught between two giant hedges. Easy to miss from the parking lot, but I knew it well. There wasn't anything special about that door, but there was truly something special on the other side.

I even had an unofficial parking spot, which I'd been able to claim for the last six months. It was adjacent to her front door and always available whenever I arrived. Like a teenager in love for the very first time, I would jump out of my car and run to her door. I would always knock, even though I knew it was safe to enter, and every knock was met with her saying, "It's open." Those two words meant *I know it's you and only you.* Those words signified safety and brought joy whenever I heard them, the same two words I desperately wanted to hear again tonight.

Upon entering, I'd find her sitting on her couch, where we shared our most intimate moments. A table nearby held two glasses and an opened bottle of red wine, setting the stage for deep and vulnerable sharing. This scene had played out for the last six months, drawing us closer in ways I hadn't imagined possible. Tonight, I hoped to revisit that scene. However, my head, heart, and gut signaled that things would be different, the fear of a potential breakup consuming my every thought and making it hard to breathe.

My mind was overrun with thoughts that this might be the last time I parked in my spot and ran to the door of Apartment 2. I couldn't bring myself to run tonight, preferring to stay suspended in time, away from the sorrow of imagining our connection's end. I thought she was my soulmate and that our broken pieces fit perfectly. We had shared every part of ourselves, or so I believed. I wasn't ready to stop exploring her mind, body, and soul. The thought of saying goodbye was unbearable.

As I pulled into my spot, the clock on my dash showed 6:00 p.m. I took a deep breath and realized I lacked the courage to knock on her door. Instead, I sat in my car and played our favorite song, "Poetry" by Wrabel. A song that once symbolized joy now echoed tragedy. As the chorus played, tears streamed down my face. Looking through my frost-covered windshield towards the sky, I pleaded with God to alter the outcome I feared yet hadn't faced.

I was raised to believe in the existence of God and that if I asked for what I wanted, He would always deliver. But tonight, under the silence of the winter sky, I wasn't so sure He would. I felt hopeless, cold, and paralyzed by thoughts of abandonment. "Poetry" played on repeat, providing a soundtrack to my conversation with God—a conversation that shifted from begging and pleading to demanding answers. These were questions I had harbored since middle school, questions that always seemed elusive yet were fundamentally rooted in one thing—love.

My relationship with faith pivots around two emotions: joy and loss. This situation already felt like a loss. I couldn't fathom why God would remove the one person I desperately wanted to grow old with. The same person I had grown to love as deeply as my two young children. She had committed to moving in this fall, a reminder she conveyed a few days earlier. I was even invited to attend her family's annual summer trip, which had been confirmed by her older sister last week. Both events suggested we had a desire to continue to build a shared future, but here I sat in such defeat.

As I pleaded with the gloomy winter sky, I wanted to believe God would hear how much this woman meant to me. "Please, don't take her from me. Please, don't do this to us, to me. Please calm this anxiety. Please soften her heart and calm her fears." I uttered the last line and desperately wanted Him to feel my emotions. I needed Him to believe what I believed—that this love was something that could last a lifetime. I wanted to trust that if God existed and loved me, He would intervene. My gaze remained fixed on the sky, hoping for His attention, yet unsure of His presence. All I knew was that I lacked the courage to look toward her door again.

Throughout my life, every time I found love, it seemed to get ripped away. What was the point of leaning in and loving someone if every time I find who I'm looking for, God and the Universe decide to take them away? I thought I finally understood how to build something real this time. The love story we were writing was the type of love that brought a rare connection—one of a kind. The woman from Apartment 2 was someone I knew I could love forever. As I sat in that parking spot, all I thought was, *how do I let go of my forever?*

I attempted to catch my breath as tears continued to fall in my lap. I felt utterly helpless. I was overcome by fears of rejection, abandonment, failure, and never being enough. These same thoughts consumed me once before and were now drowning my very being as I sat there staring at her door. I wondered how she would respond when I knocked. Would she be sitting on her couch with a bottle of wine, or at her kitchen table? I was lost in wonder while staring at the door, curious about her thoughts and actions on the other side.

I knew I needed to get out of my car. I needed someplace to go, someplace to shake off the inevitable feeling that I was about to be broken up with. My eye caught the lights of a dive bar across the street from my girlfriend's apartment. The same dive bar we often joked about walking to, even though it was the type of place that served baskets of stale bread and old packaged butter - the kind of place you don't ever actually want to walk into. Yet tonight it felt like the exact place I needed to be. The kind of place you don't ever actually want to walk into, but tonight it felt like the exact place I needed to be.

Crossing the street, I thought, *A drink or two will calm my nerves.* I entered through the side door and navigated through the crowd to the last empty barstool, feeling the Universe affirm my solitude. I slowly sunk into that tabletop barstool until a grizzled bartender would take my order. *This place was old and tattered*, I thought. The type of place that had regulars who had been coming for years, perhaps decades, yet I was the youngest and most unfamiliar face, and nobody noticed me. I was a stranger in a dive bar, and I was about to become a stranger again when I stepped into Apartment 2 to bravely face our pending talk.

As I waited for my shot of tequila and Corona with lime, I began scrolling through old text messages, getting lost in our photos and the words we exchanged. I wanted to figure out when things started to unravel so I could put the pieces back together. But scrolling through our photos was bringing on a sea of emotions. I needed a voice of reason, and the old man sitting next to me wasn't exactly the type of person to offer heartfelt advice, so I quickly dialed my best friend Alan's number, hoping he would answer.

Alan was someone I'd known for more than ten years, and he had recently met my girlfriend. Just two months earlier, the woman from Apartment 2 had joined me for a weekend in Tennessee. It was a trip to gain my friends' approval and to finally get off her couch and to someplace new. That first night in Tennessee brought a new level of intimacy and discovery, allowing us to see each other exactly as we were and to graciously accept one another despite our fears and differences. It was a journey that would forever alter the course of our relationship, and one we would fondly refer to as our "Mt. Everest."

Alan and his wife, Chelsea, immediately made the woman from Apartment 2 feel safe and welcomed, offering not just their approval but also acknowledging the special bond we shared. Given their disapproval of my previous relationship with Jessica, my fiancée, their support meant the world to me. I trusted their judgment, believing it was grounded in the wisdom of building something lasting. After all, Alan and Chelsea were the epitome of a happy marriage, the kind of couple everyone aspired to emulate because their love was apparent in everything they did.

Indeed, if anyone could navigate me through the storm of emotions I was experiencing that evening, it was them.

Alan answered on the first ring, and I blurted out, "She's going to break up with me!" Those last four words shook me to the core, or maybe it was just the word "break" that I couldn't let go of. Nobody likes things that are broken, and that's precisely what I felt as I sat alone in that dive bar.

Nobody likes things that are broken, and that's exactly how I felt, sitting alone in that dive bar.

"Hold on, Paul. What's happening?" Alan asked.

With difficulty, I recounted all the potential reasons our relationship might be ending—the reasons she might want to break up with me. It was painful to admit, but we had encountered several significant conflicts over the past six weeks, hitting a deadlock on some critical issues. Her actions triggered my fears of abandonment and infidelity, which in turn led me to react with anger and a desire to fix, or as she referred to it, "control." It had been only two months since we faced our "Mt. Everest" together. *How could we have fallen so far, so fast?* I thought.

Our most recent argument occurred just two nights earlier, but we had spent two hours on the phone discussing it, even planning our six-month anniversary. I thought we had reached a resolution and understanding, but now I was starting to question that. I understood our cycle was stuck on a loop that needed to change, but breaking up didn't seem like the answer. It couldn't be. Was it too late to repair? Could I even fix this?

Those were the questions I found myself asking Alan as I quickly drank my Corona. My hand grasped tightly around the cold bottle as I anxiously glanced at my wristwatch, trying to find stability at a time of such uncertainty. I knew there was love and lots of it, but I just couldn't shake the idea that this might be the end. I had so much love for the woman in Apartment 2, and I had always believed that love was enough to keep two people together, no matter how rocky or uncertain the journey becomes. It was the only way I knew how to love.

I stayed on the phone with Alan, drowning in sorrow and regret, as I ordered a second shot of tequila. "Is love enough to keep two people together?" I asked him. I was hoping that my friend Alan could give me some words of encouragement, but instead, he created space to just listen.

CHAPTER 2

Lightning in a Bottle

My first date with the woman from Apartment 2 was on September 11th, and I already know what you're thinking. *Perhaps we should have chosen a different date? Perhaps that was an omen from the start?* Perhaps you might be right. But after a two-year separation from Jessica and all those therapy sessions with Rick, I felt ready to try again.

I had met the woman from Apartment 2 nine days earlier on one of those silly dating apps where you swipe right or left. Right after matching, we plunged into witty banter that captivated me from the start.

Her dating profile stated, *"Basically looking for someone to motivate me to run a half marathon... Or a rollerblading buddy. Only slightly joking, realizing this is the vast weirdness of X, but definitely looking for something real. Bonus points if you're as obsessed with peanut butter as I am... or spicy food."*

She had curly hair with blonde highlights and a captivating smile that slightly squinted her brown-hazel eyes as her tongue pressed into her teeth. She reminded me of a young Keri Russell or Julia Roberts. Most importantly, she appeared honest and kind. Beyond her photos, I was drawn to two phrases: her desire to "build something real" and her mention of peanut butter and spicy food. So, considering the level of difficulty of each, I figured a fun place to start a conversation would be about the food.

Me – *"Peanut butter and spicy food? How about cashew butter and spicy food?!"*

Her – *"Cashews in a spicy stir fry is pretty fire, so I guess I can agree to that compromise."*

Me – *"LOL. Well, I'm glad we got that out of the way. The real question is strawberry or grape jelly? And toasted?"*

Her – *"Strawberry. Toasted. Even more important—coffee black or with some fixings?"*

Me – *"Definitely strawberry and toasted too. Coffee is tough; I don't discriminate. It depends on if it's drip, pour-over, French, or espresso. But regular drip coffee is usually black or with cream. You? I make an amazing French press with nutmeg, dark chocolate, and coconut."*

Her – *"Speaking my love language with that last one. Always with the fixings... used to own a French press, but now only regular drip. Hazelnut coffee is always a thing. Workout in the a.m. or p.m.?"*

Me – *"I can handle a good hazelnut, by the way. Love experimenting, though. Oat milk makes for an amazing creamer option. And coconut milk for iced coffee with curry, cinnamon, and turmeric."*

Her – *"So weird! That's an awesome combo! So basically, you're making me coffee at some point. Looking for just hookups/casual or open to more?"*

Our witty banter continued as we found common ground on both the silly and the serious. We both preferred dogs over cats, faith over agnosticism, and sleeping with a ceiling fan on. This direct and playful exchange was a refreshing departure from my previous experiences with dating and relationships. She worked as a therapist, while I had graduated six months prior with an undergraduate degree in psychology. We shared a deep passion for the field, personal growth, and self-improvement. She acknowledged "how rare and cool it was that we were both put together and both seeking the same things." The same things I had always wanted but doubted their existence—rare indeed.

Before we said goodnight, I asked if she'd be comfortable moving our conversation to text or a phone call, and then I gave her my number. She texted me the next morning, and our exchanges remained as witty and intentional as before, both of us eager to learn more about each other. I knew I wanted to meet her in person to see if our connection could be as strong face-to-face. So, I inquired about her availability for dinner, drinks, or coffee. She mentioned that having drinks would help ease her nerves on a first date, so we decided on an outdoor sushi restaurant near her place. I promised her that I would help with any "butterflies in her tummy." But the truth was, I was just as nervous and hopeful as she was.

She arrived a few minutes late, her curly hair bouncing with each step, dressed in tight black jeans, and sporting a nervous smile as she approached. Standing up from the outdoor table, I extended my arms for a quick hug. With her hair pushing into my chin, I felt immediate comfort. She smelled of sea air, and it was a cold, fall Midwestern night. She was radiant, joyful, and as nervous as she admitted she would be. We ordered drinks and dove headfirst into a conversation, connecting on many things. It was as if we had been friends for years.

The evening was filled with laughter and moments of vulnerability as we shared the lessons we had learned from past relationships—tales of heartbreak, loss, and the struggle to move on. Lessons that brought us to a place of vulnerability where we finally had to accept that we deserve better than we were given. We also talked about our shared love for psychology, personal development, and the insights we had gained from therapy. However, it was her stories about being an incredible aunt and her future aspirations that truly captivated me, drawing me in even further.

As a single father, finding someone who could love both my kids and me was paramount. Following my separation from my ex-fiancée, I spent a year in therapy and even hired a life coach. In my weekly sessions with Rick, my therapist, I came to understand my needs, wants, and desires, identifying my relationship "musts." Many of these "musts" aligned with the topics we found ourselves quickly exploring and agreeing upon. These topics ranged from tales of teenage rebellion to current and future goals and the mutual desire to build something meaningful.

I believed I was now ready to write a love story, a real one this time. And here she sat across from me, professionally in the field I've grown to love and personally in therapy herself. I wanted to believe that this meant she was brave enough to face her fears head-on and do the work necessary to grow and heal, just as I had done with Rick.

She swirled the ice in her drink, eyes intent. "Wait, slow down," she said. "You got kicked out of your parents' house?"

At 24, with nowhere else to turn, I moved in with my girlfriend, who had recently relocated to New York City to study interior design. I was hesitant at first because our relationship seemed to be stuck in an unhealthy pattern. We had broken up a few times already, and all I wanted was for her to commit. But we would struggle to make it last two more years before I finally called it quits and decided to move out. We didn't just grow apart; we had completely drifted. That city proved we were two very different people seeking very different things.

"It wasn't that I didn't love her," I explained, "but after she cheated on me multiple times, I couldn't bear the heartache any longer."

The woman from Apartment 2 was astonished. "What are the odds? I experienced something similar!" She, too, had been kicked out of her parent's house around the same time and had also fled to New York City, seeking refuge with her older sister to escape the confines of a small Indiana farm town. She was also in an unsteady relationship with a guy back home. He was a dairy farmer, and she was a college student. She devoted much of her time to helping on his farm and maintaining their domestic life while pursuing her psychology degree. Recognizing a pattern of giving more than she received, she would end the relationship after 11 years—a dynamic I was all too familiar with.

To describe our first date as serendipitous would be an understatement. It felt as though I had found my best friend, or even soulmate, someone who understood me as intimately as I understood myself. We shared childhood wounds of abandonment and mistrust, came from broken family systems, loved Billy Joel, and a desire to build something real—just as her profile read. Perhaps the only thing missing from completing our life story was one another. She was composed, courageous, and awe-inspiring, having triumphed over significant challenges. And yes, she looked phenomenal in those tight black jeans, leaving me captivated by the thought of our first kiss.

Our evening was filled with the kind of fireworks and chemistry I had thought only existed in fairytales — think *"The Notebook"* kind of connection. Cliché, maybe, but no less true. A level of chemistry that felt like a 10 out 10, like lightning in a bottle, something I had yet to experience. But on that night, I didn't have to climb a Ferris wheel to get her attention; she was already giving that to me, and I only hoped she might feel the same. As she shared her past relationship failures and her longing for something genuine, her smile would brighten, causing her nose and brown eyes to squint just a little, drawing me in even further. I was lost in her beauty, but in that moment I felt "found" in her presence.

The only interruption came when she excused herself to visit the bathroom. Seizing the moment, I hastily texted my friend Veronica as I sipped my second dirty martini, *"This chick is out of my league. I'm in awe."* My message was grammatically imperfect and perhaps a bit influenced by my emotions. Veronica's reply was swift, *"Enjoy your date. And no, she's not out of your league. She's lucky to be with you."* A beautiful reminder that self-worth and self-love should be at the forefront of all we do, that we are whole and enough just as we are. However, I was drunk from the martinis and drunk on the person sitting across from me, so those words didn't resonate at that very moment. All I thought was, *I'm the lucky one.*

I felt like the lucky one because I had yet to find any meaningful connection since I decided to date again. After spending a year with Rick, I believed I was ready to try again. But dating in a digital age often brings various experiences that had left me unfilled and hopeless—until tonight. I felt lucky because she not only listened, but was genuinely curious to learn about my story. She continued to ask deep and meaningful questions, ones that allowed me to share my journey in bravely rediscovering my self-worth by unpacking some serious events and hiring life coaches and a therapist to help me on "my own Hero's Journey."

"And what about your job?" she asked, settling back into her seat after returning from the restroom.

"I've built a successful career in sales and marketing, yet I find myself yearning for something more meaningful. I aspire to make a difference, not just sell stuff," I explained, sharing my internal conflict about my future academic pursuits. I had received early acceptance from Pepperdine to study law but was uncertain it was the right path for me. My ambition was to effect meaningful change, advocating for children and families entangled in outdated legal systems, much like my own experiences years earlier. I found myself at a crossroads between pursuing law or counseling, though the prospect of helping couples work through their issues was most compelling.

We would spend six hours sitting on the outdoor patio of that sushi restaurant, sharing with one another in a way I never thought possible. Our childhood and teenage years seemed to mirror the same storytelling as if God had always intended us to meet but instead chose to patiently wait for this September to finally bring us together. There we sat, two strangers just a few hours earlier, echoing and mirroring the same shared experiences, beliefs, values, and relationship goals. The more I shared, the more she leaned in. Her eyes intently focused on me. For the first time in 36 years, I felt truly seen and understood.

When we first recognized just how much time we had spent together lost in conversation, her eyes shifted away from me (for the first time since our date began). She quickly noticed all the servers sitting in one booth, counting their tips. We had shut the place down. We were the last table left. We immediately laughed at the thought that they would eventually kick us out and acknowledged how cool it was that they hadn't yet. I didn't want our date to end, so I quickly asked if she was comfortable with coming back to my house. I lived 20 minutes away, and it seemed like the best option for us to continue to explore one another.

Her smile was immediate, and she answered, "Yes," without hesitation.

This was not my attempt at sex, although I wasn't opposed to the idea. I just didn't want this date to ever end. After all, how often does one ever capture lightning in a bottle?

When we arrived at my place, we were caught in a moment of passion, making out as if we were two high school kids in our parent's basement. We didn't have sex that night, although we came close. It was my decision to wait: I didn't want to risk rushing anything, and I didn't want our first time to be drunk, 2:00-in-the-morning sex. I wanted to continue getting to know this brave and beautiful soul, and I wanted to make sure that I didn't end up in the "hookup category"—which she stated she "couldn't promise from happening" as she lay naked on my bed.

"I see poetry in your eyes.
You're the only reason we rhyme.
And oh my, my, my
It's a big, big, big world out there.
Been looking for something
I finally found it right here."

– Wrabel

CHAPTER 3

Warrior's Cry

I was alone in my hotel room in San Diego. The rest of my work colleagues were heading to a fancy steak house, but I couldn't join them. It had been two months since my separation from my fiancée, and I was preparing to join a Zoom call with my life coach, Brandon Clift. As I opened my laptop and connected to the hotel Wi-Fi, a wave of loneliness overwhelmed me, and I began to cry. The solitude of my hotel room underscored the isolation I felt, an isolation that awaited me at home after my work trip. I yearned for my family and hoped Brandon would offer some insightful advice.

Two months earlier, I was caught by his LinkedIn post, which included a video titled "New Warrior Training." A video filled with other men, all in peak physical condition, sharing stories of finding their inner Warrior. It could have been a recruiting video for some secret spy agency. Instead, these men were all professing how they had found the emotional healing they needed. Compelled by their stories, I decided to call Brandon and enlist his coaching services. Though uncertain about my own capacity to embody a warrior's strength and courage, I knew it was time to transform.

Jessica had moved out a few weeks earlier, taking our children with her. I was spiraling into depression, overwhelmed by grief. The storm was winning, and all I knew was that I needed more than therapy sessions with Rick to help me dig out of my current state of heartbreak and loss.

As I tried to hide my tears, Brandon interjected, "Warriors don't wipe their tears mate—they let them fall."

This piece of wisdom resonated deeply, its significance growing over time. Despite never having been married or engaged, Brandon connected with my pain through his compassion and empathy, providing a sense of safety and understanding. He was ten years younger than me but had already amassed a lifetime of wisdom. He had that all-American charm, often wearing a clean white tee-shirt over his physically fit body. His blonde hair was always combed to one side and never out of place. But he wasn't American. He was Australian. He would often refer to me as "mate," which felt endearing—especially at a time when I thought I had lost so much.

Brandon understood my pain. He was once broken. But after backpacking through the U.S., plus a stint in a South American rainforest, he had discovered spiritual experiences and lessons that surpassed any knowledge I had previously gained from any book or psychology class. He felt called to pay forward his experiences by coaching others through their own journey. He was now my guide as I embarked on my own Hero's Journey. A term Brandon used to reference the emotional and spiritual path we were about to embark on. A journey that a warrior would certainly take, but I wasn't a warrior—I felt broken beyond repair.

However, Brandon was convinced that I wasn't broken, that I just needed to heal. I needed to find a way to move beyond all the stories of my past by learning how to seek forgiveness of self and forgiveness of others. But I didn't know what that looked like, especially since forgiveness of self and others included that scary event in 8th grade. An event that I had yet to share with anyone, including Brandon. An event that forever had me stuck and confused about what a healthy and safe relationship looked like.

My Hero's Journey would bring me to the depths of my soul, sorting through many boxes that I had hidden away in my emotional basement—

boxes like safety and security, which had been violated for as long as I could remember. Unlike Rick, Brandon wasn't focused on my relationship with others; rather, he was focused on my relationship with myself. He taught me how to become a warrior for the very first time. We would spend a lot of time discussing love of self, how to receive and how to give it cleanly and safely. But I had a long way to go because I didn't fully understand self-love yet. If I had, I wouldn't be crying alone in that hotel room in San Diego. I wouldn't be navigating a separation that would have me believing that my family was now broken.

I had previously thought love by itself was enough. Love was all I ever wanted to give to someone. Someone with whom I could feel safe. Love was all I ever wanted that helpless eighth-grade boy to feel, the same boy who was never able either to shake or to share what happened to him, not even with Brandon. It was a time that stood still for me, remaining boxed in my basement, hoping I never had to confess what occurred to anyone, ever. Part of me remained that little boy who desperately sought to be seen, to be heard, and to be safe. I was now an adult, and I would show up as a giver when I found someone to love, even if they didn't know how to accept my love or give it in return.

I was hooked on unhealthy love, a love that saw me sacrificing my own needs for my partner's because I believed that was how to love someone. After all, that's what I saw within my parents' relationship. It's what my mother taught me. I just didn't know any other way to love without being completely selfless and perhaps reckless. I thought that one day if I just kept giving, I could receive that same type of love in return.

Love was my coping mechanism and strategy used to prevent abandonment and rejection. I would choose to become dependent on the very person I was with, losing all sense of self along the way. But that 8th-grade boy (my wounded inner child) would always whisper in my ear that I was broken and would always be alone, and I couldn't silence him. A wound that would play out again and again until my fears would become my reality.

As I sat with Brandon, I couldn't help but think that little boy may be right—again. I never revealed the incident from eighth grade to him. It didn't seem necessary. However, I did share the fears accompanying my transition into fatherhood. I remember the mix of joy and anxiety overwhelming me as I held my son for the first time. Born at 37 weeks and weighing only six pounds, he inherited my blue eyes. When our eyes met, I thought of all the ways I wanted to make sure he would always feel safe and seen. He was now dependent on me, but I had no idea how to be a dad or a father; I was never taught those roles, just like I was never taught how to give and receive healthy love.

I was determined to give my son a better life than my own, filled with love, joy, and security. I wanted to shield him from the feeling of a collapsing world or fleeting, conditional love. Yet, as I gazed at him, fear came over me. The fear of failure, of not being enough, and of repeating the patterns of my past. The fear that I might not know how to break free from the trauma I had witnessed growing up loomed large. But one thing was clear: holding my son for the first time meant I had to find a way to overcome these challenges. In anticipation of his arrival, I proposed to his mother and purchased a house, hoping to provide stability and hope for a future.

We built our first home in a cookie-cutter neighborhood with an HOA, a clubhouse, and numerous young families. Everything seemed perfect, momentarily allowing me to forget my troubled inner child. I dared to believe that perhaps my prayers on a lonely New Year's Eve had been heard, that failure was now a distant memory, and that life would only improve. I clung to the promise I made to God—a promise of family, a future, and being a good man, father, and husband. It appeared as though everything falling into place was a sign of divine listening, a sign that I was perhaps not as broken as I had thought. Maybe, just maybe, God was assembling the pieces I believed were missing, pieces that would complete me and provide purpose.

I was now a father and soon-to-be husband, and I had a very successful career in sales. My employer demanded a lot of my time, energy, and effort. I often traveled, spending most of my time on the road, on the phone, or in meetings. I was away from home every single week. But I was succeeding at work, which—since I was the sole financial provider—was vital. So, I embraced the stress of this demanding job because it allowed me to provide for the three of us.

I believed I was doing all the right things for the first time ever, but my commitment to work meant my availability as a dad was confined to Sundays. I had 52 days a year, outside of my six-day workweek, to navigate parenthood. Despite my success at work, I was failing at home, my greatest fear, and I couldn't figure out how to fix it.

Jessica and I argued frequently. We clashed over many issues that mattered to me, such as finances, faith, chores, and parenting. No matter what I did, it never seemed to be enough. Being the sole provider was not only a financial burden but an emotional and spiritual one as well. Jessica struggled with my lack of presence, yet she didn't work, and I was passionate about my job. I didn't want to leave my demanding employer; I sought balance and reciprocity, not in my career, but at home. I yearned for a partner who could understand my position and contribute to our life together. But I was giving beyond my ability, and it felt like she was just taking.

Our disputes became a never-ending cycle without compromise, extending to even trivial matters like TV shows or movies. We were misaligned, not just on big things but little things too, creating an unstable and uneven relationship. This constant tension made me anxious and wary, but I wasn't ready to give up. After all, navigating chaos was familiar territory for me, and we were a family—a dream I had always cherished. So, I persisted, employing the only approach I knew. I attempted to navigate being a father to one amazing little man and to find ways to stay connected to my fiancée, no matter how disconnected we remained.

CHAPTER 4

Stockholm Syndrome

Jessica and I were barely holding on as I tried my best to navigate our current challenges. I was unsure where to even begin finding ways to strengthen our relationship and end the constant fighting when she told me she was pregnant. We were expecting another boy, which meant I would soon be a father of two and a family of four. The timing of this news left me filled with apprehension. I knew I needed to be home more, so I left a decorated six-year career for a role that required a lot less travel and a five-day workweek. It seemed like the right move.

I wanted to believe this change in my work schedule would mean my fiancée, and I could finally grow together rather than further apart. I was hopeful that my new career would also provide me with an opportunity to play dad more, which meant I might finally figure out how to actually be a dad. I believed that being home more would lead to fewer arguments. Reducing one potential conflict seemed like it could help us find stability, a stability that might lead to our long-awaited happily ever after. Jessica wore a ring for four of the six years we were together, a symbol of a promise to a future that would someday include vows of forever, but that future never came.

I like to believe that we spent those six years doing our very best—which was just barely good enough. We were unequally yoked in every way. My inner child was causing me to stay in a one-sided relationship. I had grown tired of being the one who had given more than I was capable of. I felt like I had given all I could, and I eventually drifted until I lost pieces of me along the way - big pieces. The same pieces Brandon brought to my attention as he attempted to craft and chisel me into a warrior. And if you were to ask me what my boundaries for a healthy relationship were, I would have had no idea where to even begin.

As our relationship was quickly unraveling, Jessica suggested we try couples therapy. I was stuck on the belief that we weren't broken in that way. I just wasn't ready to face my shadows. I was afraid of the boxes I had hidden in my basement. Because whenever I made attempts to share them with Jessica, they were met with accusations about my past rather than an acceptance of who I am. Having exhausted every effort I could think of to fix us, I reluctantly agreed to therapy. After all, it couldn't hurt, could it?

She went straight to work finding a therapist, e-mailing me various options. We landed on an older woman who was local. She looked like an art teacher, with short, eccentric red hair and colorful earrings. I thought she was a good choice because I figured she may have the creativity necessary to think outside of the cycle in which we seemed to be stuck. Perhaps she could provide us with colorful new ways to approach our disagreements.

My father was always against therapy, claiming that therapy was for crazy people. We weren't crazy, were we? At my worst, I would become my father: stubborn, strong-willed, and physically unavailable. What I wanted to share with Jessica was that I was hesitant and nervous that this was the state of our relationship, but I didn't know how. I couldn't find the words that matched the emotions I felt inside, and simply sharing that I was scared wouldn't have worked. Jessica had high expectations for how I was to behave, and sharing feelings was not one of them.

Our therapist tried to build a connection by relating personal anecdotes, such as the challenges she and her partner faced in training their dogs, in response to our discussions about the difficulties of raising two boys. She would draw parallels between managing a household of four and her experience maintaining two homes. Despite her intentions, there was a noticeable disconnect, but since the idea of therapy was Jessica's, I remained hopeful for some positive outcome. Although she might not have been the ideal choice, she was our choice, and I wasn't ready to give up.

When prompted by our therapist to outline the issues from my perspective, I felt overwhelmed. I tried to express my desires for mutual support, emotional and financial contributions, equitable parenting, and a shared commitment to our home. However, these concerns were quickly overshadowed by Jessica's complaints about my work and the perceived luxuries it afforded me, casting me in a negative light. This framing made me seem selfish, reinforcing an imbalance I felt, but I was used to taking all the blame, so I quickly accepted her claims.

Our therapist had me believing I was the negligent one in my relationship. She quickly dismissed all my feelings, showing no empathy or desire to hear my needs—just like Jessica. Not only was my relationship hanging on by a thread, but our therapist was knitting with yarn when she should have been using a needle and thread. We needed precision and steadiness, not some oversized, itchy blanket lost between couch cushions. We needed someone who could align us and provide us with relevant tools to repair, someone who could create a safe space for both of us. But the help we received wasn't helping at all.

We both drifted. We both grew tired of trying to become people we were not capable of being for each other. We were stuck. To add to our ever-increasing dissonance, I was terminated from my new job just seven months after starting and merely five days after our newborn son was brought home. I remember sitting in the owner's office on my first day back as he explained his decision to let me go, a decision that labeled me as the problem—a position

I was familiar with. My world was falling apart, and I was at a loss for how to fix anything.

I had been laid off once before at the age of twenty-five while living in NYC during an economic downturn when job losses were common. However, this time, the reason was a vague "inability to work together." The economy was stable, but my home life was not. I recalled the emotional resilience required in NYC, a resilience I doubted I possessed now. No longer a young adult trying to make it in a fast-moving city, I had two young boys depending on me; my failure could also impact them.

My narrative of family and fatherhood was unraveling. When I returned home from my last day of work and shared the news with Jessica, her reaction was indifferent and detached.

"What did you do wrong?" she murmured, her attention fixed on her laptop, showing no empathy for my distress.

"Nothing, the owner just said he couldn't work with me. He didn't provide any other explanation. I genuinely don't know what went wrong," I responded, bewildered by the situation.

"You need to fix this. I'm not quitting school just because you got fired," she retorted sharply.

I didn't just feel broken. I felt alone. Her words cut through me like a warm knife to butter. *How could she be so callous?*—I thought. This was the woman I would marry, so I wanted to find a way to fix us, but I couldn't do it alone anymore. I didn't last very long after that. Our fights would continue and with greater frequency and conviction. We both felt unloved. We pushed and pulled at the worst parts of one another until we would eventually explode into endless and senseless arguments that never brought resolve. She needed someone to continue to support her with acts of service, and I needed someone who could provide me with quality time and unconditional love. I needed balance in a home.

Our constant cycle of fighting would continue until we finally broke. She moved out in August 2018, just before our youngest turned two. I found myself wondering, *What if that therapist was right? What if this was my fault?* As she drove away in a rented U-Haul, following her mother's car carrying our two boys, I was devastated. I stood in our driveway for what felt like an eternity, hoping she would turn around. I couldn't accept that this was how our story ended. I had always believed our kids deserved better, that we deserved better, but this wasn't the kind of "better" I had envisioned.

Shortly after we separated, I hired a new therapist for individual counseling. I would meet with Rick every Friday for an entire year. I recall crying on his couch in every session during those first three months of therapy. He wouldn't say much, just sit in his chair. When he did speak, he would ask questions that would have me pause. I wanted Jessica to be sitting on Rick's uncomfortable couch with me.

"She should be here, Rick," I said through tears, reaching for a tissue.

"But she isn't here, Paul, is she?" Rick replied.

His question felt more like a statement—a statement that would mark the start of my healing journey. Rick had the ability to meet me where I was but also gently push me forward whenever I got stuck—this was him pushing me.

At the start of each session, Rich had a cup of coffee ready for me. A peace offering that would make our sessions feel like coffee talks with a friend. Session by session, I began to understand myself better, story by story, cup by cup. Rick was masterful at helping me learn how to communicate my feelings. My favorite and most frequent was an analogy of the ocean—high tide for intense emotions, low tide for moments of stability and calm, providing a language to express my feelings.

I found myself repeatedly expressing a desire for Jessica's return. However, I eventually realized that her return was not what I truly needed. What I needed was to heal, to transform this pain into purpose. I needed to learn from this experience so I wouldn't repeat my pattern of unhealthy love ever again.

CHAPTER 5

What Burns Fast Dies Fast

A slow-burning supernova draped across the winter sky in a small Indiana town. I lived in the Midwest for eight years and had never seen anything like it before. The woman from Apartment 2 had just introduced me to her family. After I said my goodbyes and walked outside, she came running off her mother's porch with a giant smile. The same smile I saw on our first date. A smile I had grown so fond of because it was always directed towards me.

"They love you, they all love you. I don't know who you are or what you did, but everybody loves you!" she exclaimed as she took the last step off her mother's porch and leaped into my arms.

Considering her family had never approved of her 11-year relationship with the dairy farmer, earning their approval was incredibly important to me. I pulled her close as we shared a passionate kiss in her mother's driveway, marking the first time we could enjoy such a moment, making it all the more special. It was my initial meeting with her family, including her sister visiting from NYC, and her nephews and niece. I spent over six hours on her mother's couch, sipping red wine and answering their questions about my past, career, and children. I felt as comfortable with them as I did with the woman from Apartment 2.

Our relationship was still new, but that evening felt like a magical chapter in our story. As we paused from our kiss, we witnessed a slow-burning supernova lighting up the sky. An omen, or so I thought, that even the angels above were celebrating what I believed to be a true love story. The myth of a shooting star is that it will grant a wish, and in that very moment, my wish was her. I was falling for the woman from Apartment 2, just like that shooting star was falling from the sky.

I later discovered that during our first date, when she excused herself to the restroom, she had messaged her best friend, Lauren, saying, *"I think I found my missing puzzle piece."* However, it would also come to light that she had been seeing another man for months before our first meeting on September 11th. This revelation, perhaps, should have prompted me to question our situation more deeply. Yet, my conviction that I had found my soulmate, coupled with her belief in finding her missing puzzle piece, overshadowed any doubts.

While I support the idea of dating multiple people to avoid rushing into exclusivity prematurely, we were already seven weeks in when she disclosed her other relationship. I had recently met her family, who had welcomed me warmly. We'd been having the best sex of my life, and sex always meant something to me. I even began spending the night at her place, where my toothbrush sat next to hers in a cup on her bathroom sink. I didn't recall seeing any other toiletry bags or toothbrushes in her bathroom. There were no signs that she was dating anyone else. After all, if I was her missing puzzle piece, what was she still missing?

I'll always recall the moment when I first asked if she was dating anyone else. She walked out of her bedroom with this cute little prance, naked, as she stood in her kitchen. We had just made love, and she was hungry for a snack. She quickly put spoonfuls of peanut butter and cocoa powder in a bowl. She was mixing the two ingredients feverishly as she stood over her stove with a giant smile and a cute little dance. I watched all this unfold as she moved about in that tiny kitchen. I was in utter awe. The whole scene just felt like home, like something I could embrace for the rest of my life.

I envisioned our future: our kids at a friend's house while she dashed naked to the kitchen for the same snack. I couldn't stop smiling. I needed to know how she really felt about me, about us. I wanted to know if she saw the same future I did. Commitment had been missing in my past relationships, but this just felt different.

Approaching her, our naked bodies touched as I hugged her and kissed her cheek, eliciting an even wider smile. Perhaps it was the peanut butter she was reacting to, though she often said she felt safe with me.

I embraced her for a moment before I courageously asked a question that had been on my mind since meeting her family, "So, are you dating anyone else?"

She paused, then deflected with, "Are you?"

I quickly assured her, "No," but added, understandingly, "But if you are, that's OK. I know that's part of dating." My heart was racing.

She began to share with me how she had been "sort of seeing some guy," who she was "dating before we even met," so it's not like she "was actively dating or seeing anyone else." She explained how she was "thinking about ending it anyway," and added the footnote that they were doing "everything but intercourse," so I "didn't have to worry about anything like STDs or feeling like it was cheating."

Her revelation was unexpected, but I wanted to understand, so I patiently stood in her kitchen as she continued to share. Initially, I thought dating others was a pretty logical, safe, and healthy response. After all, isn't this how adults are supposed to date in this modern digital age? Although surprised, I wasn't discouraged. I had hoped we were exclusively building a future together and had no interest in seeing others. However, I refrained from judging her uncertainty. I guess I should have asked this question sooner.

Shortly following this conversation, we deleted our dating apps and began the start of a committed and monogamous relationship—or so I thought. Following the official start of our newly defined relationship, she would often share with me how she was "waiting for the other shoe to drop" and would follow up by asking, "How are *you* so sure about this?" Those two questions have remained etched in my memory because I now believe those were the very questions she was asking herself. It never mattered what my answers were; they would never have calmed the uncertainty that was already nestled inside of her.

She was, after all, recovering from an 11-year relationship. One in which she could never be her full self, one her family didn't support, one that taught her the virtues of taking things slowly and the danger of a good thing spoiled over time. I accepted her story because I had also found myself caught in a similar fear. I had spent six years with Jessica, so I could only imagine what 11 must have felt like for her. I was compassionate, empathetic, and understanding of her need to move slowly. So I didn't panic—at least not initially—when she shared her hesitation about jumping in with both feet.

The story behind the end of her 11-year relationship was rooted in heartbreak and loss and explained why she was "waiting for the other shoe to drop." It was a story I chose to accept. That other shoe had become a symbol of what our relationship eventually grew to become. And, on my 37th birthday, after three months of dating, the woman from Apartment 2 showered me with thoughtful gifts and a beautiful card that read:

"So excited to see what this year brings for you, and just pray it's nothing but blessings & goodness! I seriously am so grateful for you, and just hope you know how much you mean to me—Also, I figured I'd let you keep 'the other shoe' this year and decide if you want to drop it versus me."

Her thoughtful card was complemented by my favorite gift from that night: a golden key chain with a pendant in the shape of a high-heeled shoe—a token that she had not only dropped her other shoe but was letting me keep it for the rest of the year. I interpreted it as a gesture of her trust in me, in us. It brought a moment of pause. I recall sitting, staring at the pendant, before my eyes moved back to her. That keychain and heartfelt note made me believe she was willing to suspend her doubts and emotional uncertainty and embrace the unfolding potential of our relationship.

On my 37th birthday, her shoe not only dropped but was placed in my hand, with care and with permission to decide if I was the one who wanted to give it back. The truth is, I would have held on forever. It was easy to give her all the time in the world to decide when she felt safe and ready to go all in. After all, I was her missing puzzle piece, and she was my forever, and when you find your forever, all you really want to do is hold on. When she gifted me that card and that silly little keychain, the world stood still for a moment. My love, like that keychain, was something I never wanted her to let go of.

However, that keychain and clever card foreshadowed the events to come. What she really wanted to communicate was her uncertainty and fear of trusting in someone, anyone. She wasn't just "waiting for the other shoe to drop" because of past experience. She was waiting for something bad to happen, something that would validate her need to run to a place of safety, to never be stuck in a derailed relationship again. "Waiting for the other shoe to drop" was a euphemism for saying, as well as she could, that she was not capable, willing, or able to ever go "all-in." I had been here before. And yet, I didn't recognize it this time.

*"Don't forget to make all these little things individuals—
all of them special in their own way."*

– Bob Ross

CHAPTER 6

Get a Shovel and Dig

I n eighth grade, I was sexually assaulted by a sophomore in high school. Someone I thought was my friend. His father was our baseball coach, and when our season ended, my new friend invited me over. My "friend" was a cliché: your typical all-American boy, tall, strong, athletic, well-known parents, and a bright future, on and off the field. I was two years younger than him, with half the talent and popularity, so I felt important when he invited me over to his home. I felt wanted—like I mattered.

Until the day he handcuffed me to a pole in his basement.

This assault occurred at a time when I had already started to question everything. I was questioning who God was and what my relationship with Him was supposed to look like. I was questioning my father's values—his religious beliefs and the conservative ideology he forced on me, which insisted people can't be trusted and that the world is a cruel and evil place. I was questioning why my parents fought all the time and why all my friends from grade school had become so mean. I felt so alone. All I knew was that puberty was occurring at a rapid pace, and I was already not comfortable in my new body.

I struggled to interpret how this type of event could occur and why I failed to stop it. *Did I allow it to happen? Did it mean I liked it? Did this make me a bad person? Was I gay? Was I bisexual? Would I go to hell?* All those thoughts and more flooded my young brain. But I chose to suppress them, burying them deep down in my soul's basement, never telling anyone about them. I would place them in a box marked *"Do Not Open,"* and that's where they would stay because it never felt safe to share them. I knew I couldn't tell my parents, especially my father, because my father had always told me that sex before marriage was a sin. Sinning meant I was going to hell. Hell sounded like a lonely and scary place, one where love could never exist.

That following fall, I entered high school. This is a time in every adolescent's life when the distance between child and adult quickly diminishes. Seniors and juniors driving cars meant freedom was within reach if I could just hang on. Letters on jackets separated the cool kids from the outcasts, and the jocks and athletes were favored not just by gym teachers and cheerleaders but by all teachers. This should have been a time when I could grow up, too. But I didn't feel like I was growing up; I felt broken and confused.

I had this belief that adults didn't allow bad things to happen to themselves. Adults were supposed to have it all figured out. I didn't even know where to begin because I wasn't sure what I could safely share anymore. My body was taken from me, and so was my voice. I remained suspended in time, bound to the feeling of being tied to that pole, the feeling of his mouth on me. I didn't like any of it, but I couldn't stop the scene from replaying over and over again.

I continued to reason that if I told my parents, they would blame me for what occurred. And I couldn't handle the shame and guilt. Unable to share the pent-up hurt, I remained numb and lived inside an insecure shell for all four years of high school. I walked those hallways and convinced myself that it would be OK again one day once I got out of there. But those four years brought even greater adversity. I was seen as a loner or troublemaker, frequently getting sent to the principal's office, taunted by my peers, and judged by most teachers.

I was the class non-conformist, and one of very few. It wasn't that I didn't want to fit in; I just didn't know how. I was so scared to interact with the popular kids because I might risk being seen by my abuser. So I choose to be different, to dress differently, and to identify as an outcast. Being an outcast meant I could have a small group of friends who were outcasts just like me. That small group felt safe because I didn't have to be seen by anyone else. We were the group that everyone else tossed aside, judged, and condemned. Many of us carried a lot of hurt from our experiences, but we were never mean to each other.

I walked those hallways in a black hooded sweatshirt with a golden zipper, metal studs lining the sleeves, and a hood that was also covered in safety pins and various punk rock patches. My hood was always up. It became my safety net and prevented others from fully seeing me. That hooded sweatshirt would quickly become tattered, torn and overworn—a symbol of what I felt inside. Just a year earlier, I was the nerd in class, and now I dressed differently, which caused concern for my parents.

I felt broken, and so did most of the other outcasts. They, too, had broken homes, stories of abuse, and felt unseen, unheard, unloved. We always made each other feel safe because we intimately knew that underneath our studs, tattered hoodies, and painted nails, we just wanted someone to love us exactly as we were. We just wanted to be enough. But it was easier not to fit in with most kids: not fitting in meant I never had to communicate those needs, wants, and desires with most people.

My freshman year of high school also coincided with the infamous Y2K propaganda. A story circulated across all forms of media that machines would fail to recognize the year 2000. We were fed a narrative that the world would stand still for a moment and eventually come crashing to an end. I thought to myself, *If the world ends, will I go to hell?* My mind raced. Would I never experience a love story? Why did everything feel so heavy all the time? I wondered why God would allow me to exist if the world was going to end. More importantly, why did he let that sophomore break me beyond repair?

I thought of my father's strategy for surviving the end of the world - an event he often prophesied and promised would come. A strategy that I believed would leave me hungry and alone, a sinner, stuck in my parent's basement with a bucket of rice, a few bottles of water, and a shotgun. Those items were the essentials my father would purchase online to ensure we could survive the impending doom—items ordered from the same machine that would somehow fail to recognize the year 2000 and see that I was condemned to hell for all eternity. But his strategy didn't sound like survival to me, and it certainly didn't feel safe. It wasn't the life I'd ever wanted to live. After all, who wants to just survive?

I wanted to live. I wanted a life filled with joy, safety, and love. I wanted a life of meaning, a family of my own one day, and if I was stuck in my parent's basement fighting over the last bottle of water, what was the point of surviving? Nothing made sense anymore. I would turn 14 just a few days before New Year's Eve. I can't remember anything about that Christmas or even my birthday. However, I vividly recall that New Year's Eve and the persistent feelings of hopelessness and abandonment that ensued—emotions that would become all too familiar.

That night, as my parents slept soundly, I lay awake in the bottom bunk, overwhelmed by a sense of impending doom. Maybe if the world survived, I could finally tell them what occurred. Perhaps, they would accept me and understand me. Perhaps, they would finally see me for who I was. I also wondered, what if they wouldn't? What if they would continue to reject me by choosing to shame and guilt me for something I never even wanted to occur in the first place? The one benefit to the situation, I reasoned, was that if the world ended, I would never have to reveal anything to them.

The ball dropped, and the lights remained on. The world seemed to survive this doom—I never understood how. But while the world survived Y2K, I had never felt more scared and alone. That night, my confession wasn't with my parents; instead, it was with God. I didn't ask him to forgive me, necessarily, but I did want to share with him what was in my heart and in my head. I figured if I was about to become an adult and actually grow up, I should get things straight with the big guy upstairs.

As I lay awake in my bed, I made a vow to God to strive for a better life, one that would make Him proud. A promise that I would try and figure out how to do this thing called life. A life that included dreams of a family, a loving marriage, children, and a commitment to goodness despite knowing all my hidden struggles. But it seemed as though God didn't hear me, just as He hadn't when I stood outside Apartment 2 on March 12, desperately seeking divine intervention. Because just a few years later, I would feel stripped of any future promise yet again.

CHAPTER 7

Valentine's Day

Winters in the Midwest can be unrelenting. "The Lake Effect" often brings freezing temperatures and ungodly amounts of snowfall. My first winter with the woman from Apartment 2 proved to be no different. That year marked the record for the most snowfall in Northwest Indiana in 42 years, which meant date nights with my girlfriend were now cozy evenings at home. However, I didn't mind. For me, this meant more time spent on her couch, sharing bottles of wine and stories.

We maintained an ongoing list of topics to discuss, which we referred to as "pins." These were opportunities to revisit conversations that either lacked closure or needed further exploration. Recently, our pins included deep dives into past relationships and former flings. She frequently inquired if I would ever consider reuniting with the mother of my children, questioning if I still harbored feelings for her—a reasonable question, considering our six-year history and daily communication for co-parenting.

I promptly answered, "No," but she pressed further, suggesting it was acceptable to admit lingering feelings. As a therapist, she believed she understood the complexities of co-parenting relationships and was convinced that some level of connection and desire for reconciliation would always exist. However, I was content with our separation and valued our co-parenting arrangement. Yet, I felt she sought more than a simple denial.

"If you're asking whether I'd welcome back the mother of my kids in an ideal scenario, the answer would be 'yes' because I never envisioned raising children with someone who wouldn't be part of my life permanently. However, she has personal issues to address, and I doubt she's willing to confront them," I explained, hoping this would reassure her by highlighting the unrealistic nature of such a scenario. My aim was to maintain a healthy co-parenting dynamic for our sons' sake, yet my explanation seemed to heighten her anxiety. Perhaps my message wasn't conveyed as intended, or maybe it didn't align with her expectations.

My affection for her wasn't solely sparked when I saw her dance in her kitchen with peanut butter and cocoa powder; I had been captivated since our initial encounter on that brisk September evening. We shared the same love languages—quality time and physical touch—further cementing our connection. And whenever we spent time together, our bodies collided in bursts of lust and passion. We got lost in every room of her apartment, completely naked. Those were the moments I wanted to replay and recreate for the rest of my life.

But even if I had communicated better, would it have ever made a difference? *Could* she be assured by anything I could say?

As Valentine's Day approached, I thought perhaps I could demonstrate to her how much she meant to me and re-instill her confidence. What is the holiday for, if not to celebrate love stories that bring deeper joy and romance? That's exactly what I wanted to build with her: something with depth, something that would last. While discussing how we would celebrate, I didn't feel the need to focus on the Hallmark superficiality of candy and flowers because we already had a love story that far exceeded that. But I still wanted to celebrate with her because she was worth celebrating.

However, she had a different idea. She expressed a wish to spend Valentine's Day with a friend. Her friend, Lauren, had recently become single

THE WOMAN IN APARTMENT 2

and "couldn't handle being alone on Valentine's Day." I strove to be understanding of this request, not wanting to seem selfish or overly attached. My anxiety was already heightened by a remark she made a month prior, suggesting "she couldn't love the way I love." Above all, I believed the specific date of our celebration was less significant than the joy of being together.

We decided to observe Valentine's Day on February 12th, coinciding with the day Jessica, the mother of my children, moved from Illinois to Tennessee with her boyfriend. This farewell to me and our sons (who were now living with me) made February 12th significant. It was also the day I had planned to get a new tattoo along my left rib cage:

> *Fate whispers to the Warrior*
> *You cannot withstand the storm*
> *And the Warrior whispers back*
> *I am the storm*

This new tattoo was symbolic of many things. It was a reflection of everything I had overcome—or so I thought. It was also a reminder of all the lessons learned from my life coach, Brandon, just two years earlier—lessons that helped me understand that being a warrior includes the need for strength and the grace of acceptance. I now understood why warriors let their tears fall, and I wanted to print this poem on my body so I could tell anyone who asked what it meant to me.

I believed in the power of storytelling, and the story this tattoo held couldn't be any closer to the heartbreak, loss, and fears of abandonment that I had always felt. It was an opportunity to finally stand in victory in all that was and to embrace all that is. I thought this tattoo was a unique way to let go of my past because I was now creating a beautiful new future with my girlfriend, a special love I hoped would last as long as that ink on my skin.

Little did I know the tattoo would become a continuous reminder I needed for myself.

February started off in chaos. Jessica insisted on stopping by, a request I was more than willing to accommodate, but it had snowed the night before, and the roads were a mess. She arrived late and tracked snow throughout my home as she headed for the back door and toward the garage. She wanted to get the last of her boxes that I had kept while she was in transition. She loaded her car, waved goodbye to our boys, and left as quickly as she had come.

Once she left, I immediately started my Jeep and began to back out to head to my tattoo appointment, but the moment I did, I got stuck in three feet of snow. I sighed with frustration. *Why doesn't our town plow our alleyways?* I thought. I did not want to be late to my appointment or worse, miss my first Valentine's Day with my girlfriend. I needed a quick fix.

Reaching for my phone, I called Jessica and asked if she and her boyfriend would help. Considering they had just left, I hoped they were close enough to lend a hand. It took them and three generous neighbors to push me out. Once freed, I quickly drove off, hoping for the best. My stomach growled: I'd had no breakfast and little coffee, and I was discouraged about how the day had begun. I was uncertain what this move meant for my boys and unsure what it would look like to attempt to co-parent from such a distance. But I didn't want to get lost in those thoughts—there was plenty of time to sort those things out. I wanted to focus on the present, this exciting night that my girlfriend and I had planned.

She was aware that the mother of my boys was moving and had asked lots of questions, wanting to know how I felt about Jessica moving so far away. I mentioned I was a bit worried about how the move would affect our boys but felt okay overall. Jessica's relocation had been in the works for months. She'd moved a few times before, but this was going to be the biggest leap yet. My girlfriend's request to spend Valentine's Day with a friend seemed genuine, and I was thankful for our ability to share openly and honestly with each other.

She met my boys in early November and hit it off with them instantly. She'd always check if they could stay up late to play upon her arrival. She filled our home with laughter and delight as they played hide-and-seek or built forts in their bunk beds. Witnessing their bond filled me with happiness, and I was hopeful for more moments like these, especially with plans for her to move in by summer's end. So, despite some worries about Jessica's move, the comfort and love my girlfriend provided them gave me a sense of reassurance.

Heading to the tattoo parlor, I received a text from my girlfriend, suggesting a talk that night about a "pin" she wanted to discuss. I hadn't expected it to involve past relationships, given my ex was en route to Tennessee, and we were set to celebrate our relationship that evening. Expecting an intimate conversation, I eagerly agreed, optimistic for our future and our first Valentine's Day together.

As I gritted my teeth, listening to the buzz of a needle etching the wisdom of a Warrior into my raw skin, the anticipation of our evening—filled with both intellectual and physical intimacy—occupied my thoughts. Our conversations had always deepened our connection, reminding me how fortunate I was to have someone so eager to delve into every aspect of my being.

After the tattoo session, I hurried home, packed an overnight bag (forgetting my pillow), and set off for her place. Successfully navigating the unplowed roads, I found my usual parking spot. I scrambled over a snowbank, snow and ice seeping into my socks and shoes and rushed towards her door. I eagerly knocked (as I always had), and she responded, "It's open" (as she always did).

Inside, the flowers I had ordered were the centerpiece of her kitchen table. But she was the centerpiece of her apartment, sitting at her kitchen table in a beautiful piece of teal lingerie. Teal, the same color she'd often wear as eyeliner, which always made her beautiful brown-hazel eyes pop. Rose petals on the floor led to her bedroom, with a bottle of wine and two glasses set on the table, one already filled for her. Her beauty and the thoughtfulness of the setup took my breath away. No one had ever made Valentine's Day so special for me before. I took a moment to soak it all in, wanting to etch this scene in my memory forever.

She remained seated as I quickly kicked off my shoes, scattering bits of snow across her apartment floor, my socks wet. Tossing my winter coat onto her couch, I moved closer, but she stayed in her chair. Kneeling down, my hands softly brushed over her pale, freckled legs. As I kissed her stomach and looked up, our eyes locked. With our gazes fixed on one another, I expressed how beautiful she was and how grateful and thrilled I was to be with her. She had always felt like home to me.

Standing back up, I reached for the open bottle of wine, poured a tall glass, and took a big sip before sitting down. She felt distant, and I sensed that her desire to talk was at the front of any thoughts she may have, so I asked her to share her pin.

She waited for a second, then leaned in. "I need to understand the relationship you have with Jessica because it feels like friends. And if it's friends, I don't think I can do this relationship."

Completely confused, my heart beginning to race, I responded emphatically, "We're not friends."

"But you are."

"Look, she's the mother of my kids, and there will always be care and a need to co-parent, and I want to see her do well, but it isn't *friends*."

"But it is," she quickly retorted, defending her opening statement.

I was bewildered. *Was this her way of letting me know she wanted to end our relationship? Today of all days? What was the purpose of the rose petals?* I wasn't brave enough to ask any of those questions, but before I could respond, she continued:

"It's kind of like the boundaries you asked me to set with Isaac and Corey."

"I'm not sure boundaries with an ex-boyfriend and a guy you met at a bar are the same as boundaries for the mother of my boys."

"But they are," she stated with a cold, level stare.

She and Isaac had met for drinks shortly after we became exclusive, and she'd told me of their meeting only after it occurred. This was the same man she had dated for three months, with the relationship ending seven months before we even began. She withheld this meeting from me because her friend Lauren convinced her to keep it a secret. Lauren felt I didn't need to know about it, which didn't make me feel very safe. She didn't seem to have a pattern of making good decisions in her own life, and I worried why my girlfriend would think it would be acceptable to keep a meeting like that from me.

Corey wasn't an ex-boyfriend or even a former fling, just someone my girlfriend met at a singles bar two weeks earlier when she and Lauren went out for drinks. She had told me that she was going out to be a "wing-woman." But the night was a little more involved than that. When the bar closed, they were invited back to Corey's house to continue the party. Lauren hooked up with one of Corey's friends, and my girlfriend ended up at Corey's home, talking with him in his kitchen until 4 a.m.

She would eventually confess to me that he had flirted with her but that it "felt safe." She shared that even though he had hit on her all night, he was now a friend. She was adamant that he was "just a friend." But that didn't seem like any type of friendships I made. It all felt very unsafe to me. It felt like betrayal—absent of any trust. This is certainly not something I would consider doing, but maybe we were just different in this way.

I wish I could have listened better, but I struggled as she tried to establish the correlation between those two men and my co-parenting situation. I couldn't understand why she would even bring this up, especially on a night like this. I thought it was apparent how platonic my relationship with the mother of my boys was. It was a business relationship. We weren't friends: friendly, yes—but not friends.

Friendship is defined by reciprocity, and our relationship had always lacked just that. And because our boys were so young, I believed they needed to have two parents who were still involved in their lives. I wanted them to understand that just because their mom and dad were separated, this didn't mean we were broken. Jessica felt the same. But my girlfriend didn't. She felt anxious, and perhaps that was why she thought I didn't have any boundaries when I thought I did.

This was supposed to be a night of romance, but this wasn't the type of intimacy I had in mind. I wanted to get lost in those rose petals with her. Instead, she stayed focused on the need for boundaries. She insisted on reasons for keeping Isaac and Corey as friends, even though their behavior and desires proved to be anything but. Perhaps this was why she was sensitive to any form of friendship she believed I had with the mother of my boys. I wanted to understand, but the more she brought up those two men, the more hurt and triggered I became.

We were lost in a conversation that was rapidly squeezing out any room for compassion or empathy. She was half-naked, rose petals were strewn on the floor, and both of us were drunk on wine, yet we were completely disconnected from one another. I wanted her to trust and understand my need to have a healthy co-parenting relationship. But *friends*? What difference did it even make?

At its core, I was confused and hurt because I felt she didn't trust me. Trust is a foundation of safety, and all I wanted was for us to feel safe again. I wouldn't be sitting in Apartment 2 with the woman I believed to be my soulmate if I had any doubts about our shared future. I wasn't doubting what we were building, so why was she?

I don't think I can do this relationship. The phrase wouldn't leave my mind.

All that raced through my head was, *How do I fix this*? I just didn't see any way out.

The trauma from my past, which had taught me that love was transient, was suddenly at the forefront of my mind, overwhelming me. The thought that we could erode just as quickly as we began was flooding every single fragmented thought. My heart raced uncontrollably, each beat louder and more forceful than the last. But my focus wasn't on calming my breathing; it was fixated on her, on us. In that moment of silence, she climbed into my lap, seeking intimacy, but I couldn't reciprocate. I turned my face away and toward the floor, my hands falling from her waist.

I couldn't shift my emotions that fast. All I wanted was to be heard, not touched in a way that felt like a distraction from that need. It wasn't that I didn't want to make love to her the moment I walked in and saw her in that teal teddy. I did. I was just stuck on the single frame of abandonment and rejection. Emotions that reminded me of that 8th-grade boy who was voiceless and helpless, handcuffed to a pole, and unable to say "no."

By leaping into my lap and attempting to make out with me, she made me feel used, like cheap sex. I didn't want a physical experience with her but a soul experience. I wanted to make love to her. But I couldn't communicate those words, so I sat there numb and emotionally distant, trying to make sense of what just occurred. But I couldn't put the pieces together. Everything seemed so confusing, so scattered. My words weren't enough, but hers were. Her words exploded inside my heart and head like fireworks ringing in a New Year. I felt completely helpless.

Misunderstood and misguided emotions sabotaged a night of romance that never came to be. We sat in silence before finally deciding to call it a night. She knelt to pick up the rose petals, tossing them in the trash. I slowly moved to the floor to do the same. Seeing those rose petals tossed into the trash was symbolic of the events that just occurred. It felt like my love was trampled on and tossed away without care, and I imagined she felt the same.

When we finished cleaning up, she went to the bathroom to change out of her lingerie and into shorts and a tank. I gathered my overnight bag from her living room, walked through her kitchen, and took a deep sigh. *How did things go so wrong?* I was unsure if we were still together. But all I wanted was to stay and spend the night with her.

She was still in her bathroom when I entered her bedroom so I placed my toiletry bag on her nightstand and changed out of my distressed gray-washed jeans. I carefully tossed them to the side and removed the extra pillows from her bed. As I tossed the last pillow to the floor, she entered the room from the bathroom and made one more attempt at connection. Playing a country song on her phone, she took me in her arms to dance with her. But I couldn't dance. It wasn't that I didn't want to. I didn't know how, not after hearing, "I don't think I can do this relationship."

She felt rejected, and I felt abandoned. Our first Valentine's Day would end very differently from how I envisioned it. Setting our alarms for the morning, I prayed that it would bring clarity and reconciliation. We said goodnight to one another, and I pulled her close, not wanting to let go. Her body pressed into mine, giving me hope for the morning, but my heart still hurt. I wasn't sure how we could overcome a night like this.

I learned that heartbreak doesn't always come at once; often, it comes in pieces, like rose petals scattered across a floor. Moments when the relationship slowly starts to unravel and erode, often without any apparent logic or reason. The lonely feeling of being in bed with a soulmate who has already drifted kept me stuck in a state of abandonment until we would eventually break.

"Love is not a constant of knowing, and there will never be any guarantees. Love is a continuous process of discovery and unfolding."

– John Kim

CHAPTER 8

Love over Fear

In my senior year of high school, I sat in a gymnasium with my classmates as my high school gym teacher pointed to the sobering images on the TV. He began shouting, "We're being attacked, we're being attacked!" The Twin Towers in New York City had just been hit by a plane, and the world stood still yet again. The words *"Terrorist Attack!"* scrolled across that TV screen. I immediately thought of that shotgun and bucket of rice and wondered if they would serve a purpose now.

Completely hopeless, voiceless, and consumed by fear, I felt—yet again—like life could be taken so easily. My father's words echoed in my head: "The end is near," just as he had proclaimed during Y2K a few years earlier. I watched in horror and confusion. This time, it felt like my father got it right. I wasn't sure if I should look up to the sky and pray or just run and hide. Senior year of high school would become a complete blur. I couldn't separate my own unaddressed trauma from the trauma of the nation.

When my parents would ask what college I was going to or what my plans were once I graduated, I would freeze and feel my chest tighten. *College? Plans?* I never even thought those were options. I was still clinging to every experience those four years had brought, which proved just how fragile the future could be. Every day, I'd wake up to my dad watching the news on an

88-inch tube TV that dominated our living room. The channels would incessantly update us on whether it was a yellow, orange, or red day, signaling the risk level of another attack.

Those colors were an indicator of the level of risk for us being attacked again. Every day was a constant reminder that the world around me could disappear at any moment, a reminder that instilled an increase in fear and uncertainty. I suppose I should have been excited about graduating and picking a college. But, the truth was, I wasn't even sure how to survive the day, let alone any thoughts of a future, and those damn colors weren't very helpful.

That year, I spiraled, living as though each moment might be my last. I didn't exactly make the wisest choices. I sought refuge in music, drugs, and alcohol—anything to numb the overwhelming feelings that my late teenage years were engulfed in. The trauma that anchored me in place wasn't a continuous saga of abuse but rather vivid flashbacks. Moments of an eighth-grade me, handcuffed to a pole in a basement, my dignity stripped away by someone I considered a friend. Snapshots of lying awake on New Year's Eve, anxiously watching the ball drop, half-expecting the world to end, and now I was witnessing horror unfold on every screen while grappling with questions about college and a future I never believed I'd have.

That last year of high school was supposed to be a year when I had it all together and all figured out, I thought. A year when I was supposed to know what I wanted to be when I grew up because growing up was still possible. Everyone else seemed so confident in the direction they were going, and I couldn't understand how that could be. Hadn't we all experienced the same things? Even my friends in their tattered hoodies would receive college letters of acceptance. But I was stuck, with no direction or certainty.

CHAPTER 9

I AM

G rowing up, I would have described my parents' relationship as chaotic. When my friends asked if they were still together, I would always respond, "Yes, but they shouldn't be." Divorce seemed so common, and the kids of those divorced homes seemed so much happier than me. I could never fully understand my parents' relationship. How could two very different people ever stay together?

My parents fought often. Explosive arguments over mundane things like helping with groceries or who was to watch my brother and me. Considering we never spent any quality time together during the week, I dreaded weekends. They usually involved my dad rising at dawn to spend the whole day outside, tending to his prized lawn. He took immense pride in it, always talking about his perfectly manicured grass.

He'd wander the yard barefoot, a screwdriver in one hand and a bucket in the other, meticulously removing weeds. To him, those weeds were public enemy number one. The neighbors' admiration for his impeccable lawn didn't help either. It was as if his yard had leaped straight out of a *Good Housekeeping* magazine. Witnessing his obsession, I figured this was what adulthood entailed, and I wanted no part of it as I grew up.

My mom was the polar opposite. She was always on the go. She never stopped moving long enough to walk barefoot on the lawn like my father did. She couldn't. She was the one who managed all the things inside of our home, juggling errands and shuttling us to our various activities—just the three of us, since Dad rarely joined. Although we kept busy, our family rarely felt connected.

My father was rigid, unforgiving, and very authoritative. His determination was evident in his desire to achieve outside the home, often prioritizing the lawn and our family's outward appearance over my feelings. He constantly had a list of chores for me, and that list was always in place of anything I wanted to do with him. My childhood was governed by his stringent rules and an endless list of chores that stripped away the joy of just being a kid.

His list would include things like cutting the grass, cleaning his tool shed, cleaning the pool, or shoveling buckets of gravel and rock. This was all before I was allowed to hang out with any friends. It wasn't exactly child labor, but it was far from an ideal childhood. Initially, I tackled these chores with the hope that completing them would free up some of my dad's time for us. But the list was never-ending; no matter how much I accomplished, he always found more to be done.

I grew up believing that hard work and acts of service were the only paths to my father's love and approval. The rare moments I spent with him involved pulling weeds on his precious lawn while my peers enjoyed swimming or summer camp. Everyday after school and every summer for years I would be stuck on that lawn, his lawn. I was so busy chasing after his love and attention that I believed this was the only way to receive love from others.

My father sought to instill his view of the world in me not by asking but by telling. He was utterly inflexible. If anyone disagreed with his opinion, it would be an argument to the death. There was never any winning in discussion with him. Eventually, we all learned to tap out or just avoid it altogether. I'll never forget how often my dad would say, "You can't trust anyone." Meanwhile, my mom seemed to have love for everyone. Dad saw the world as a place full of selfish takers, while Mom was the ultimate giver, offering endlessly regardless of how little she received back. She embodied the idea that it's okay to give and never said no to helping others, no matter how exhausted she was, so neither did I.

In her efforts to keep the peace in her relationships, including with my dad and me, she'd avoid conflict at all costs. Her anger, when it did surface, was unlike my father's blatant fury. Hers was more childlike, manifesting in defensive lash-outs, guilt-tripping, or shaming. It wasn't a healthy response, but I didn't recognize that then. She unintentionally taught me to believe that I would risk being left or abandoned if I ever communicated my true feelings or stopped giving to others, so I learned to box things up and keep them in my emotional basement.

Growing up, my parents were often emotionally and physically unavailable. Sure, they did the best they could. But their behavior left an imprint on me since childhood. An imprint that taught me that love equals chaos. An imprint that taught me that nothing good would ever last or ever be safe for very long. An imprint that taught me that love was unapologetic, conditional, and distant.

As an adult, I was now trying to learn new ways of communicating and confronting conflict in healthy ways. I had to learn the difference between healthy and unhealthy attachment and the difference between dependence and codependence. I had to relearn how to give and receive healthy love. I had to find the courage to heal. I had to look inward and find the courage to share. I had to be willing to grow beyond what my parents taught me in order to become something more. I had to find peace knowing that I was enough just as I am.

I didn't have to repeat what I saw growing up.

Chasing after love had become my trauma response to all the shit that happened to me when I was growing up. I overcompensated by loving even when it was no longer safe or healthy to do so. I was so scared of losing love that I'd cling to it, always attempting to fix what wasn't mine to fix. My interpretation of love would prove to be very different from my partner's. Maybe that is because I was raised to believe in a God who loved without condition, a Christian God who sent his only son to die on the cross for me. It all seemed a bit complex to understand as a child, so I assumed that's what love was: a great sacrifice. I assumed it was OK to hurt.

I didn't just love the woman from Apartment 2 unconditionally. I loved her *sacrificially*. When her actions caused me to feel anxious about her commitment to our relationship, I would respond by giving even more love despite my well-being and safety. I would sacrifice my needs, placing hers above my own. I would continue to give this type of love until I had nothing left to give to myself. This would lead to a pattern of unmet expectations and subjugation. I found myself stuck in unhealthy cycles of fighting, cycles that would have a resolution (or so I thought), but never addressed the core issue: my desire for reciprocity, safety, and to be seen.

Because my understanding of love was different from my partner's, we would be speaking two different languages when we said, "I love you." We were expressing two different kinds of love for each other yet using the same words. The misunderstanding of what we each meant created gaps in the connection and intimacy we tried to establish. There's a vast difference between "I love pizza" and "I love you." If someone doesn't share the same definition of love as me, their "I love you" might as well mean "I love pizza"— a form of love lacking any deep, soulful connection, focused on the object rather than the essence, devoid of depth.

These gaps hindered our ability to truly see and hear each other. They left a void in our connection and compromised our sense of safety with one another. We weren't cultivating a genuine, intimate bond because we were both holding back. We couldn't fully reveal our true selves, trapped by fear rather than empowered by love. Despite any chemistry, we remained disconnected, lacking a solid foundation to rely on during challenging times. Our relationship was like a structure built on sand, inevitably washed away by the tide.

As the prospect of commitment became more real, she continuously sought reasons to doubt its safety and the authenticity of my love. She frequently questioned, "How are you so sure about this?"—a question I found difficult to answer convincingly. No matter how earnestly I tried to convey the depth of my love, she remained skeptical. It was then that fear began to take hold. That silly voice that starts as a whisper:

*"She doesn't **really** love you."*
*"She's **cheating** on you."*
*"She's **lying** to you."*
*"She'll **leave** you."*

Fear is a monster. It's only goal is to destroy, not build.

When fear became my emotional driver, I grew anxious, and the woman in apartment 2 became avoidant. All I needed was her to validate that she loved me too, that she wasn't leaving. But her actions were starting to prove otherwise, and I wasn't sure how to soothe the voice inside my head that kept insisting she was going to run. It didn't help that our ability to communicate was at an all-time low. Her need for avoidance and my need for assurance caused me to chase after her in an attempt to fix our relationship, to pull her close. This push/pull dynamic became our dance for the last few weeks until we stopped dancing altogether.

Sitting alone in that dive bar would mark the beginning of my healing journey. A journey I thought I had conquered post-breakup with my fiancée when I learned how to become a warrior. Brandon provided me with new tools and blueprints for building a healthy relationship with myself and with others. The same lesson Rick was teaching me when he asked what my boundaries were. Beyond those coffee sessions with Rick, my coach, Brandon would push me to further explore my relationship with my parents. He helped me to become conscious of my parents' behaviors and taught me how their behaviors would become the *masks* (these metaphorical masks were the learned behaviors I picked up from my parents as a kid) I would choose to wear.

Having a mother who struggled to emotionally connect made me gravitate towards emotionally unavailable women. These women would shy away from conflict, resorting to guilt and shame, and would abandon the relationship at the first sign of trouble—mirroring how my mom treated her friendships. My father's strict adherence to rules instilled in me a tolerance for rigid, unforgiving, and controlling behaviors in others (father mask). He equated love with conditions and chaos, always placing the blame on me when things went awry (father mask). Thus, I became a fixer, and despite his warnings against trust, I swung to the opposite extreme, wanting to trust everyone.

My parents taught me that the only way to behave in a relationship was to embrace the chaos. To sacrifice my needs by serving the other person (avoidant mother/mask). I was led to believe that marriage would only ever be, at best, *good* enough. This belief is why I would settle for lopsided and one-sided relationships. In my romantic relationships, I would default to codependency (caretaker), selflessly serving others and putting my partner's needs ahead of my own (avoidant mother/mask). This dance would become the unhealthy patterns of sacrifice, fix (rescue) and control that I would replay subconsciously on my partner. It was a vicious cycle and one from which I knew I needed to break free.

When I was processing these pieces with Brandon, I was still grieving the separation from my ex-fiancé, the issues with my family, and a future that never came to be in my therapy sessions with Rick. I allowed myself to get consumed by high tide. High tide had become a frequent wave of emotion that would drown my very being. I would find myself sitting on the floor of my shower crying, completely paralyzed by sadness, and unable to move. High tide was when my entire being would become so consumed by abandonment, rejection, and loss that any hope for a joyous future seemed like an impossibility.

I recall relying on one of my closest friends during a time of high tide. My friend Veronica encouraged me to create and to celebrate "small wins." She believed I needed to create small moments worth celebrating. But I had no idea how because I felt so broken. I felt I'd failed as a father and a partner. I struggled to get out of bed because I could no longer face the person in the mirror. Veronica clarified that, sometimes, simply getting out of bed and showering would count as a small win.

"Just focus on achieving those two things, nothing more, and then celebrate them," she added, "Just get out of bed tomorrow and promise me you will shower."

I wasn't sure where I would find the courage to do so. I avoided the shower since most of my showers would include sitting on the shower floor, bawling, and pleading with God to bring my family back. I didn't understand the purpose of the separation. But, a few days following my discussion with Veronica, I woke up and immediately went for a shower. For the first time in months, I didn't cry. And when I got out, I finally caught myself smiling for a moment—not because I was happy, but because I felt that small victory Veronica encouraged me to achieve.

Stepping out of the shower, I stared into my bathroom mirror. I grabbed a black Sharpie from my bedroom desk and wrote the scripture from Psalms 147:3 on the foggy glass: *"He heals the brokenhearted and binds up their wounds."* It was at that moment that I understood I wasn't alone, that God understood heartbreak. Perhaps he hadn't abandoned me after all. I continued writing until that mirror was covered from top to bottom:

I AM A FATHER

I AM A LEADER

I AM ABUNDANCE

I AM STRONG

I AM A SON OF GOD

I AM A SERVANT OF GOD

I AM WORTHY

I AM ABLE TO RECEIVE

I AM READY

I AM GROWTH ORIENTED

I AM A STUDENT, READER, LEARNER, AND TEACHER

I AM GRACE AND GLORY

I AM LOVE

Those words would become my mantra every morning, in every shower, and every night before I went to bed. I would read those words aloud and with conviction. I wanted to feel them in my soul. They would become the words that I rebuilt myself on until I believed I was worthy and until I believed I was loved. Every day, I would find myself gaining greater confidence in reading those words, and every day I cried a little less.

"Traumatized people chronically feel unsafe inside their bodies:
The past is alive in the form of gnawing interior discomfort. Their bodies
are constantly bombarded by visceral warning signs, and, in an attempt to
control these processes, they often become expert at ignoring their gut
feelings and in numbing awareness of what is played out inside.
They learn to hide from their selves."

– Bessel A. van der Kolk

CHAPTER 10

Mt. Everest

Starbucks in hand on a cold Friday morning in the middle of January, my mother had arrived early to babysit. My oldest was on his bus and off to school, but my youngest was home, bouncing off the walls. He was too young for pre-school and had only two settings: play and eat. This often made working from home a bit challenging. Navigating Zoom meetings would include ducking and dodging as Nerf darts came rocketing in my direction. I knew my mom would have her hands full, but she never seemed to mind.

My mom had become the coolest grandma ever. She was affectionate and generous, always coming over with snacks and gifts. I trusted her with my kids, and they loved her deeply. They would never let her leave without at least three hugs. My youngest would remain on the porch waving goodbye when she left, refusing to return inside the house until she was long out of sight. She even let them make messes without having to clean them up right away. This was one way her role as a grandma was different from what I had experienced of her as a mom. She took things slower and remained more in the moment.

"Grandma's here! Grandma's here!" shouted my youngest as her car caught his attention.

I was excited for my mom's arrival, and even more so for the extra coffee she had picked up for me, running on only four hours of sleep. I became so busy the night before, putting together the perfect playlist for my upcoming road trip with my girlfriend, that I lost track of time. Three days together in Nashville was more than just a nightly sleepover at apartment 2. It would be the most time we would spend together since we started dating. My girlfriend was a little nervous about the prospect. But I wasn't. I was hoping this trip would deepen our connection.

Perhaps my confidence was rooted in the holiday and New Year's celebrations. Granted, we had yet to spend three consecutive days together, but we had spent a lot of time with each other and each other's families. I had grown to love her family and the time we spent together. They showered my two boys and me with Christmas gifts and welcomed us with open arms. Watching my kids play with my girlfriend's nephews and niece brought immense joy, amplifying the happiness that had filled our homes over the past few months.

Shortly after my mom arrived, my girlfriend showed up. I greeted her eagerly in the foyer with a hug and her favorite Starbucks drink, a white chocolate mocha. My youngest son tried to squeeze in between us, eager to play, but we had a long car ride ahead and a dinner commitment to keep. After ensuring my mom was set, I packed the car with our bags and bid farewell to my mom and son as we embarked on our journey.

The drive to Tennessee from Indiana was a long straight stretch of interstate that includes two lanes and many windmill farms. The landscape could easily have led us to rely solely on our playlist, but we never got to it. My girlfriend had other plans, retrieving a book by Dr. John Gottman from her backpack. We had both read his book, *The Seven Principles for Making Marriage Work*, which includes various assessments and exercises designed for couples to explore through safe, scripted dialogues. One such exercise, the "Love Map," involves quizzing each other on intimate details like preferences, dreams, and fears.

She opened to that section, challenging me to see how well I knew her. With every question, I answered confidently—I didn't need to cram for this quiz. My affection for her went beyond the physical; I genuinely cherished learning everything she had shared with me. Somewhat surprised by my responses, she smiled, impressed by how well I knew her. That set the tone for the rest of our drive, filled with deep conversation reminiscent of our chat outside the sushi restaurant after our first date. This level of intimacy was something new for me, reinforcing my belief that what we had was truly special.

As we neared Kentucky, the scenery shifted from windmills and dairy farms to bridges and glimpses of city life, and our conversation took a heavier turn.

"I'll always love him; he'll always have a place in my heart," she said, referring to her ex, the dairy farmer. I was beginning to think he was the reason why she had waited for the other shoe to drop, the same shoe she had gifted to me a few weeks earlier on my birthday.

"I know," I said as I gently placed my hand on her leg.

With her eyes moving toward the passenger windshield, she continued, "He's getting married in the fall. On the same date we had picked for our wedding. I know he's doing it just to get back at me. It's like he wants *me* to know."

She started to cry quietly, her gaze fixed on the passing countryside through the dark passenger window. That moment of silence was the only pause in our six-hour drive. The only sounds were her soft sobs and breathing, and it was the only time I considered turning to my playlist. But I didn't. I chose not to interrupt this moment of emotional release; sometimes, offering silence is the greatest support we can provide. Instead, I just sat in silence with her. I felt her pain and heartbreak, and I wanted her to know that it was ok.

Truthfully, I would have taken this pain from her if I could have. I wanted her to know that I would do anything for her, but this wasn't the first time she confessed the feelings she still had for him. *Was she capable of loving me while living in her past?* I thought. However, I wasn't brave enough to ask that question.

My anxiety began to grow. I questioned whether her emotional hesitancy was a barrier that time could erode or if it would remain a permanent fixture between us. This silence brought me back to a conversation we had on her couch a week prior, where she expressed her difficulties with being monogamous.

"The thought of never being with a woman ever again makes me sad," she added. That scene kept replaying in my head as we sat in that growing silence.

A few minutes would pass before that silence was broken by her voice.

"Let's talk about something else, ok? Tell me all about Alan and Chelsea!" she said as she wiped her tears away.

I smiled, grateful she was interested in my closest friends. "I'm pretty sure they'll greet us with big hugs and cocktails. Get ready for some fun!" I assured her.

Upon reaching Alan and Chelsea's, their warm welcomes and tall martinis were just as I had predicted. After the long drive, it was the perfect greeting. Alan assisted with our luggage as Chelsea led us to the kitchen, arriving just in time for dinner. We spent the evening around their kitchen island, sharing cocktails, playing our favorite songs, and dancing like carefree college students.

The drinks flowed until our dancing slowed, but with Rufus still playing, I asked Alan to join me outside for a cigarette. He wasn't a smoker, and neither was I—unless I was drinking. Honestly, I wanted a moment alone. Before we could stumble out of his front door, I drunkenly asked with enthusiasm.

"So, what do you think?!"

"Man, she's great. Chelsea and I love her!"

It meant the world to hear those words because I felt the same, and I trusted Alan. I trusted in his understanding of love and how he saw it in others. I admired what he and Chelsea have; it gave me hope that love between two people can exist. His marriage was the type of marriage I wanted to have. Knowing that Chelsea and Alan approved helped instill a confidence that her love for her ex-boyfriend, and my own insecurities, might not break us after all. But I wasn't ready for the events that came the moment we returned inside.

CHAPTER 11

Trauma Triggers

At 7:30 p.m. on March 12th, after one Corona and two shots of tequila, I crossed the street toward Apartment 2. That dive bar had served a purpose: to numb any and all feelings that I was about to be met with by my current (but not for much longer) girlfriend. That short walk felt like an eternity. When I finally got to her apartment, I took a deep breath, as if knowing this could be the very last time I approached the door of Apartment 2. I paused for a moment, then knocked. "It's open," she replied. The same two words I had been met with for the last six months. So, I opened the door and walked in with a bit of hope.

Upon entering, I quickly scanned the room as she was exiting her bathroom. I noticed a bottle of wine on the kitchen table had already been opened, and there were two empty wine glasses next to it. *Two, not one. That must be a good sign*, I thought. Perhaps there was a reason to be hopeful after all. As she walked close to me, I reached out to hug and kiss her. She shrugged off my attempt at affection and politely asked if I wanted a drink. Something felt off, and my heart began to race. I immediately felt hopeless, voiceless, and rejected—my old triggers.

I responded with the only words I could muster: "I've already had a few, thanks though."

"Should we sit on the couch or the floor?" she asked.

"You're most comfortable on the floor, so let's sit there."

My response was honest. It was one I believed to be true. Even though her couch had brought with it many intimate conversations, it was when we moved to the floor that I sensed her walls lower. The floor was where she'd first confessed she'd had another meeting with Isaac. She'd met with Isaac to give and receive closure for a three-month-long relationship. But his motivation was for a second chance. She invited him back to her apartment that night, where he continued to confess his feelings, attempted to spend the night, and even kissed her. She recounted this story with me over the coming weeks and would often downplay the kiss or even deny that it had ever occurred.

"You are the one who told me about the kiss," I was finally able to courageously remind her.

"I guess I tell you more than I remember when I'm drunk," she said, sitting on the cold laminate floor of her living room.

I was hoping for that same outcome tonight, not for discussions about ex-boyfriends or another rehashing of defenses for her behaviors, but rather for the remembering piece. I hoped she would remember how much we loved one another and perhaps have a change of heart. So, I thought her floor would be the best place to begin. I took a deep breath and looked down at my shoes. They were still on, and so was my jacket. It was as if my body had already understood that I was no longer welcome here. Perhaps I would be leaving soon. Perhaps I was already a stranger in Apartment 2.

I knew our conversation was about to be very different from what I had hoped and prayed for just a few hours earlier. I sat across from her, my shoes and coat still on. Our eyes caught one another's for a moment before she turned away. She started to cry as she began, "I just can't do this." At that very moment, I felt abandoned by God, by those shots of tequila, and by my now ex-girlfriend. But I wasn't ready to let go of her just yet. So, I did my very best to hold on as she continued to share.

"We have all these beautiful pieces. You're everything I've always wanted. I just can't do the fighting. It's too triggering for me. We can be friends, even friends with benefits. I just can't do a relationship with you."

My mind raced as I listened to these crushing and confusing words. *Friends? With benefits?* What did this even mean, and why was she giving up?

I was too blind and too love-drunk to accept the words: "I just can't do the fighting." Perhaps those two shots of tequila and that one Corona from that dive bar where nobody knew me had abandoned me after all. When she finished sharing, I hung onto those six painful, yet simple words: *"I just can't do the fighting."*

She was right; we had been fighting, but our fights were always rooted in fighting for the relationship, not against it, I thought. I struggled to understand her need to stray outside of monogamy and her desire to hold onto ex-boyfriends and retain them as friends. Ex-boyfriends like polyamorous Jeff, whom she would still make out with. I struggled to understand why she was still receiving unsolicited and inappropriate messages from men with whom she wouldn't set any boundaries. I struggled to accept that Isaac and Corey were viewed as friends when, to me, they felt like a threat to our relationship.

While we fought over those needs, I didn't think they were enough to break us. But she struggled with our avoidance and anxious themes—her words not mine. She felt my boundaries with the mother of my children were too lax, and my anger or what she perceived as controlling behavior made her feel unsafe. My frustrations weren't in danger; rather, it was a desperate attempt for her to see the reasons for setting boundaries with "friends" like

Isaac and Corey. Yet, the boundaries I proposed felt "yucky and gross" to her, leading to her resistance and my heightened anxiety and desire to control. It was a relentless cycle, lacking compromise or mutual understanding.

I never imagined these things would lead to our downfall. I thought of all the ways to communicate and convey my belief in what we were building. I wanted to convince her to not let go and to hold on. But, instead, the only words I could get out were, "Please don't do this." Four lonely and insecure words that sounded just as they felt: desperate. Maybe the tequila had deserted me, just like I feared everyone eventually would. I couldn't let go, unwilling to face another break.

I began to debate against her sober decision to run, arguing from my love-drunk and Tequila-fueled perspective for why we could repair what was broken, but it wasn't working. My desperate attempt at convincing her to stay went against her well-rehearsed reasons for needing to run. She had not only built a wall, but she had also already run. I was trying to run toward her, but I couldn't run through the emotional wall she built. Was this the same wall she built when other guys got close? The same wall that already shut me out before I could even share how I felt? Did it matter?

I sat there for a moment as tears filled my eyes, but this time, I let them fall. I thought about how alone I felt just a few hours earlier when I begged and pleaded to that gray winter sky. Perhaps God didn't hear me after all? Or maybe he just didn't care? I thought about the story we had been building, a story that would rival *The Notebook* and any future Ryan Gosling movie. I was the first person her family approved of, and that meant something to me. To me, it meant that we were meant to be together.

Our families adored seeing us as a couple. I fantasized about seeking her hand in marriage. We shared dreams of a future home—a modern farmhouse with ample land for stargazing by a bonfire while our children slept peacefully. Our visions of the perfect wedding aligned, down to exchanging identical

Pinterest inspirations. We even shared the same chosen name of a future daughter who would never exist. We were aligned in so many ways. Why would she choose to run? All those memories of a shared future came crashing in. High tide was here, and I was drowning in a sea of emotion. I felt completely broken.

"Broken" was a word she hated hearing and a word I thought I overcame. But I didn't know any other word to describe what I was feeling, and I didn't just feel broken. I felt shattered into a million pieces, like dust scattered across her living room floor. I begged her to give us time to work through these differences. I begged her to give us a chance, to try again. I just couldn't understand why she was throwing in the towel when we were leaning into the resources necessary to learn and grow beyond our current state of friction.

We had just wrapped up our fourth session of couples therapy, and it felt like we were barely scratching the surface of our issues. Our puzzle pieces, once fitting seamlessly, were now colliding and clashing, echoing a cycle of feeling unseen, unheard toxicity born from our deep-seated fears of betrayal and abandonment. Therapy was our chosen path to healing. I was all in for fixing what was broken between us, but she was looking for the exit. I believed healing our traumas could eliminate the triggers that made a relationship seem impossible to her. It felt like we were so close to overcoming this cycle, yet here she was, choosing to let go.

This was the stage of our relationship that could have determined and defined the type of love we were giving one another. Mine was unconditional beyond measure; hers was conditional, with clearly drawn lines for anger and control and some scribble around monogamy. Perhaps this is what she meant when she said she "couldn't love the way I love"? Her boundaries were both non-existent and visibly scattered.

When relationships move beyond the honeymoon stage, both people are stripped bare. They become fully exposed and vulnerable, generally for the first time since the relationship began. At this stage, each person will inevitably trigger the shit out of each other. I'm not talking about leaving the toilet seat up or dishes in the sink; I'm talking about the stuff we put away in our basement and mark "do not open."

These are the same boxes we don't ever want to share with anyone because those boxes are filled with our trauma. The same trauma that will always remind us of all the shit we don't like about ourselves. All the shit our parents taught us, all the masks we choose to wear, all the triggers from childhood. I thought I had identified all my boxes when I was working with Brandon and Rick. But at that very moment, I understood that I must have missed something; I must have overlooked a box that needed to be forgiven.

We both failed to courageously speak up for the type of relationship we needed and wanted to build until it became too late. Until she let go.

When she stated that she couldn't be in a relationship with someone who triggered her, I sat there confused. She seemed to believe that she could find someone who wouldn't ever trigger her. But triggers are not a reflection of our partner; they are a reflection of our past. They remind us of the work we must choose to do, not of the partner we push away. We all have trauma, which means we all have triggers. Trauma is a growing part of the human experience.

I'm not advocating for anyone to remain in a toxic relationship involving physical, emotional, or verbal abuse. However, I do think that triggering each other is a natural phase in any relationship. It's an opportunity to look inside at the boxes we've buried and identify all the pieces in our basement. When a relationship calls for greater intimacy, we will always trigger each other with the stories we are sharing. But if we choose to walk away at the first sign of discomfort, we'll never discover what could have been. How can we expect to open up about our deepest fears and not trigger our partners at some point?

There I was, tequila on my breath, desperately pleading for her to stay in a situation she simply couldn't endure because I was clinging to the past and unable to face the present reality. My own traumas had me stubbornly trying to make the woman from Apartment 2 stay. I didn't want to become abandoned again, especially by a woman I was convinced I would grow old with. But we both had pieces that we failed to work on before coming together.

In a final effort to make her reconsider, I said, "You do understand you're chasing an illusion, right? That kind of person you're looking for doesn't exist."

"I know……" Her response was soft, her eyes brimming with tears, mirroring my own.

At that moment, I understood her need to be authentic and affirming. She knew she was seeking something that didn't exist, but she stood by the very idea that it could. I, too, was once seeking something that didn't exist, which kept me stuck in a six-year one-sided relationship rooted in the idea of One Day. But, my One Day never came, just like her perfect partner never would, either. She needed to let go of this fantasy, but she was unwilling. Even though she was crying and equally as heartbroken, it was a decision that felt right, just for her.

I sat there on her floor for what felt like an hour, emotionally naked, sobbing like a child, my heart in her hands as she was handing it back. She had already let go.

"All of us, at some time or other, need help."

– Mr. Rogers

CHAPTER 12

Ashes to Ashes, Dust to Dust

Seven weeks into our relationship, I spoke of my desire to be exclusive. When we both agreed to exclusivity, I didn't think there was a need to further explore relationship definitions with her. What we should have discussed was how we each defined monogamy. But, shortly after we committed to one another, I learned more details about her sexual identity and dating history—a history that included a polyamorous relationship, bisexual experiences, and difficulty in letting those pieces go. She confessed all these needs, but I insisted that our love was enough.

When she walked me through her polyamorous dating history, it included a relationship with two people, her friends Samantha and Jeff. She shared with me how she had ended their relationship when the topic of children came up. Jeff wanted her to have their child, and her response was to run, as she always did when a partner leaned in.

Though this was very different from my experience and expectations of relationships, I didn't run when I first heard this story. Instead, I sat and did my very best to understand. But while I didn't run, in hindsight, perhaps I did retreat just a little because following this story, I certainly started to drift to a place of anxiousness and fear. My inner child panicked as she bravely shared with me this most intimate part of her past and her identity.

Maybe my perspective seems out of step with today's world, but I hold onto the belief that it's possible to find that one person to craft a lasting love story with. That's what I yearn for—a partnership with someone who doesn't seek distractions or entertain temptations from outside our bond. I thought that was what we were creating together. I thought I had love figured out this time. But I now started to wonder if perhaps my view no longer existed. *Was I wrong for wanting monogamy?*

I spent a whole year sitting with Rick on that uncomfortable couch, learning about my needs, wants, and desires. I even learned what my relationship "musts" were—musts that included love, safety, and connection, because those had always been the deficit to anything I had yet to experience. But I had never learned what existed outside of my list.

I bravely dove headfirst into healing that wounded inner child when Brandon guided me through my own Hero's Journey, or so I thought. I've had various sexual partners that brought with them various sexual experiences. Yet, I find myself wanting vanilla, and honestly, I believe vanilla is very much underrated, underserved, and underappreciated.

The thought of seeing my girlfriend with someone else, regardless of their gender, didn't appeal to me at all. I wanted to understand her perspective but realized I wasn't fully listening. She was asking for exceptions to be made and to redefine how we defined our relationship without using those words. We sat on her couch as she continued:

"Isn't that every guy's fantasy, to see two women?"

"It's just not something I can experience," I replied. "Not with someone I love."

Her disappointment was palpable. I realized I wasn't courageous enough to delve deeper into the conversation. I was letting her down by not meeting her needs, and I was betraying myself by not standing firm on my own desires for monogamy. The timing of this revelation was particularly tough for me. I had hoped my love would be enough, that she wouldn't crave anything beyond what we had. Yet, I should have realized she also sought the freedom to explore relationships with women.

Our trip to Tennessee took a turn when she hooked up with a woman, afterward admitting that "my love scared her" and that she "couldn't love the way I love." I wasn't hurt by seeing her with a woman, although I wasn't fully comfortable with it either. But I was devastated by her comment about our different kinds of love. *How do I love differently so she isn't scared?* I asked myself.

Overcoming that series of events is why we often referred to that trip as our "Mt. Everest." It should have broken us, but somehow it didn't. Not right away, at least. When we first walked through that event, I thought it was our peak, and perhaps it was, but it was the descent I wasn't ready for. It wasn't that I didn't love her exactly as she was. I truly did. I understood that she was bisexual and accepted this part of her. I didn't realize, however, that accepting this piece meant needing to make an exception for her to remain intimate with women.

Asking me to accept her need to still be with women felt like a huge difference in values. I thought we were very much aligned in our expectations and values. But this one felt different. These negotiations were being thrown my way in a matter of months. At the same time, God and the Universe kept reminding me of the synchronicity and chemistry we shared, so I wanted to hold on and find a way to make her happy. I wanted to find a way to accept all these pieces without casting any judgment or shame, but I didn't know how.

A year spent with Rick on his uncomfortable couch, creating uncomfortable moments for discovering my boundaries and drinking too much coffee, instilled a belief that I was capable of loving someone again. I thought I finally understood what love actually looked and behaved like. I thought the love I was now giving was enough to sustain and build something real. But it wasn't. I began to wonder if my love really did scare her.

Truthfully, I like vanilla with sprinkles, and she liked assortment, and I just couldn't end up being one scoop on a giant sundae and ever feel like enough. I neglected to prioritize self-love and embrace my own needs and preferences, which are essential to defining who I was and am. Once more, I found myself caught in the cycle of codependency—a cycle filled with pain, loss, and heartbreak. That's what happens when I let others hijack my purpose and violate my boundaries; the outcome is always pain. I believe hurt people hurt people, and we were both hurting.

Following our breakup, I spent months dwelling on our past relationship, fixating on everything I could have—or should have—done differently. I often thought through all the ways I could have listened more; all the ways I could have stopped trying to fix (control) things. I revisited that specific conversation on her couch, where she revealed her desire to be with women and my reaction to it. I couldn't forgive myself for how I handled it.

This was one scene that I wish I could have revisited.

I would often ask myself, *What if I just accepted these pieces within her? What if I was OK with unethical monogamy or polyamory or whatever flavor of ice cream she wanted to have? What if the title she needed to put on the relationship in order to be seen and heard was something I could actually be OK with? What if I could stop being so hurt, scared, and angry? Why was I trying to control this free spirit when all she wanted was to love others? What if my love didn't scare her? What if it was OK that she loved differently than me?*

Maybe my ego just couldn't handle her need for straying.

The agony of dwelling on all those "what ifs" stems from the conditioning and patterns I encountered growing up, coupled with the

THE WOMAN IN APARTMENT 2

trauma that convinced me love was synonymous with chaos. All the trauma that prevented me from ever seeing red flags in this or any past relationship.

Like trauma, red flags don't always have to be a big or recurring event. Sometimes red flags can show up as tiny little events that compound over time. Small insignificant events like tiny little landmines buried deep inside my heart, spirit, and mind until they inevitably scatter me to pieces. That's how it felt when the woman from Apartment 2 stated that she could be "friends or friends with benefits," but she "just can't do a relationship." It's a feeling of dust, completely shattered into a million tiny little pieces, and how do you ever put dust back together?

"Careening through the universe
Your axis on a tilt, you're guiltless and free
I hope you take a piece of me with you
And there's things I'd like to do
That you don't believe in
I would like to build something
But you never see it happen."

– "Motorcycle Drive By" by Stephan Jenkins, Third Eye Blind

CHAPTER 13

Be Brave and Authentic

T he days and nights moved slowly following the breakup with the woman in apartment 2. I remained numb to everyone around me, including my kids. I was on auto-pilot, trying to navigate a newness I didn't want. A newness that meant I lost someone I love. A newness that brought with it a whole world of sadness and misguided emotions as I would argue with myself and everyone else that the love we had was real. I would attempt to convince anyone who would listen why she would return one day. But nobody was buying my reasons for wanting to stay.

The sounds of joy that once filled my home were gone. Whenever my youngest asked me to build a fort or play hide-and-seek, I'd always find a reason why I couldn't. Every activity that reminded me of my now ex-girlfriend felt like a sharp reminder of what I'd lost. She was gone, and I couldn't bear the thought of playing those games without her. My youngest would often end up building forts alone while I hid in the bathroom to cry, not wanting my children to witness my constant sorrow. However, even as a toddler, my youngest was aware of why I was sad. As their father, I knew they deserved better from me. I knew I needed to heal because if I stayed broken, it was only a matter of time before they broke too.

Rick's uncomfortable couch was now weekly sessions by phone. I sought his guidance once again, knowing I couldn't face this heartbreak alone. In our initial session, I poured out all the reasons I felt I had failed and why she had walked away. I was convinced that the end of our relationship was related to my anger and our conflicts—the very issues she had pointed out as her reasons for leaving. I thought if I could fix those pieces, the same pieces she couldn't handle, maybe she would return.

"Do you remember your deal-breakers?" Rick inquired during one of our sessions.

He knew I had recently outlined new deal-breakers and was now testing my recall of them.

"I do," I responded confidently.

"Number one is my favorite. Do you remember that one?"

"Yes, I do."

"What is it?" he coyly asked.

I hadn't memorized my deal breakers yet, and Rick knew it. But before I could confess, he followed up with another question.

"I wonder if your deal-breakers would work with her."

I didn't want to answer, so I sat in silence. It reminded me of when he asked what my boundaries were. I thought he might be proud of my ability to craft such clearly articulated deal breakers, and ones with meaning—ones that exceeded my previous list of relationship musts. Yet here I sat in my backyard, unsure of everything, as my kids joyfully ran around. I couldn't even recall the first one. In that growing silence, I thought of what it would look like to not have that short list of deal breakers. Deal breakers like not tolerating cheating, and I went right down that rabbit hole of "what-ifs."

I didn't want to accept any of it, so instead I asked my own question: "Do you think she'll ever come back?"

I was desperate and afraid. Afraid that I'd lost my soulmate forever.

I didn't yet trust in my new boundaries or deal-breakers, so I had to learn the hard way. I was tangled up in unresolved trauma and a pattern of codependency that manifested through my romantic relationships. I was doomed to repeat this cycle until I confronted that scared eighth-grade little boy, assuring him of his worth, acknowledging his fears, and recognizing his capacity to heal. I came to understand that those carrying unresolved trauma often appear as beautifully damaged souls, much like that younger version of myself—a beautiful, broken soul representing my wounded inner child, the shadow driving me toward unhealthy relationships.

The painful conclusion of a love story highlighted what truly matters in cultivating a healthy, secure relationship. Heartbreak and loss weighed heavily on me as I clung to the memories of passion, love, and connection with the woman from Apartment 2 long after she had moved on. I couldn't come to terms with the fact that our shared dreams and the life we were building together were over. I struggled to accept her reasons for why she chose to build a wall and run. Her final text message to me was a plea to stop reaching out, to let go, but I was at a loss on how to do that.

I wondered how it was so easy for her to set such a harsh boundary for me, especially when she had resisted setting similar boundaries regarding her exes and past flings. The thought of blocking people made her feel "yucky and gross," yet she seemed to dismiss me without hesitation. I held onto the hope that the right words, if I could just find them, might reignite our connection and pave the way for reconciliation.

I struggled to find a way to just "be" at night, when all I wanted was her body next to mine. I couldn't find peace in an empty bed. I attempted to find ways to fill the silence of nighttime with an emotion other than sadness, but it was difficult. I had to stop playing my iTunes playlist titled "Date Night" because it always reminded me of her couch, wine, and our intimate nights when our bodies collided. I had to take showers and never sit down because I would often become paralyzed and consumed by sadness when I did. I had to consciously think a little less of what was and instead find joy in what is. But until then, I felt broken beyond repair. I was drowning in the grief.

My weekly sessions with Rick couldn't come soon enough. In each session, he always provided me with a nugget of wisdom on which to reflect. In the coming weeks, he shared with me that "losing a loved one is worse than a death because they still exist but are no longer with you." I'm not sure if that's true, but I do know that learning to let go of the woman from Apartment 2 certainly felt like both.

The grieving process became a storm of emotions, which I believe can weaken the strongest person and bring them to their knees. And until I got up, found a shovel, and dug deeper, I would stay stuck replaying that damn highlights reel, convincing myself that I could have somehow changed an outcome—an outcome that we never had any control over in the first place.

"And if you were with me tonight, I'd sing to you just one more time."

– Jimmy Eat World

CHAPTER 14

Kid Thinks He's Gonna Drown

I found myself crying on my shower floor, in my car, and over my stove, as I struggled to make breakfast. This pattern occurred every single day for months. When I reached for my phone, I often played my iTunes playlist titled "Date Night." That playlist reminded me of her cute little dance and her love of peanut butter and coffee with all the fixings. Songs in that playlist included "Poetry" and "If You Want Love" by NF, which always triggered feelings of love and loss. Songs can attach us to a single event in time, with the power even to rob moments of joy.

"If You Want Love" will forever remind me of the moment I found myself crying in her bed for the last time. We'd spend the night, morning, and afternoon making love to one another. It was as if we already knew we would never see each other ever again, but our bodies and souls fought to stay connected. When morning hit, I gently woke her up. I wanted to make love to her one last time, but I paused. Reaching for my phone, I played "If You Want Love." It was my attempt to emotionally dance with her, to communicate how much I love her, since all previous attempts had failed.

When the chorus hit, we both cried hysterically in her bed. She was as heartbroken as me, but she couldn't stay, and I couldn't do friends with benefits. We eventually moved to her kitchen, where I had my last cup of "coffee with the fixings" that she would ever make me. I sipped it slowly at her kitchen table. She wasn't in lingerie this time. There were no rose petals, just two broken hearts that didn't know how to say goodbye to each other.

"My heart wants to stay, but my head is so conflicted," she said as she cried in her kitchen chair. I felt so helpless. I wasn't sure what to say or do. I wasn't sure how she could be so conflicted—still. I didn't need anyone to confirm that all I wanted was for her to stay.

"Then don't do this. Don't let go," I pleaded as I held her hands in mine.

"I don't want to, but I just need some time. We can try again in six months."

I hung on to that promise of trying again. A promise I believed in. But here I was now, alone, trying to put together all the pieces of our now-broken puzzle. Yes, I had Rick again, but I had so many unanswered questions that I wanted to ask her. The longer we were apart, the more I reflected and learned, the bigger my questions became. I dived into numerous books about relationships, trauma, and self-love. While some offered healing, others only intensified my guilt and shame for how I had behaved. These books all pointed out our flaws—hers and mine—but left unanswered whether love alone was enough.

The pain of her silence was unbearable. Slowly, the message sank in. I began to think the silence would last not just six months, but forever. I couldn't sleep. I smoked too many American Spirits, listened to many sad songs, and got lost in the few pictures of us that I had left in my phone. I had deleted our text thread the morning following our breakup. She asked me to delete our intimate pictures, and I thought it best to just delete everything. It was so important to me that she felt safe, always, even in that moment.

Since I was never taught the difference between healthy and unhealthy love, I relied on artists like Stephen Jenkins and films like *The Notebook*. They shared a common theme: a chaser (portrayed as avoidant or hard to get) and

94

a runner (the anxious pursuer). I grew up believing that healthy love involved chasing someone until they decided to stop running and stay. I thought love was all you needed. But The Beatles lied to you and everyone else. "All you need is love" is a f**king lie. I needed more than love; I needed someone like Rick, and to find self-love and self-worth.

I needed to understand what was lacking in my concept of love. I had to come to terms with the fact that love alone isn't enough to persuade someone to stay or give things another try once they've decided to leave. I had to redirect my energy and calm my anxiety with every text notification—each one igniting hope it might be her. I had to stop revisiting old messages, even those that celebrated our connection and hinted at a future together. Those messages only fueled my sadness and the narrative of what could have been, forcing me to confront the reality of what was.

After Jessica and I split, I clung to the notion that I had somehow failed at love. The thought of enduring the loss of love and feeling broken again was unbearable. I doubted my ability to withstand another heartbreak. Yet, when I met the woman from Apartment 2, I discovered the courage to love once again. When I told her, "I love you," I meant every word. Yes, it was scary to think that she could leave me. But I assured myself we were different from how Jessica and I had loved. When we started to drift, it was as if my body knew before my mind. That's why sitting in that silly dive bar brought such a rush of scary and familiar feelings.

When the woman from Apartment 2 found the courage to share more with me than anyone else, I responded by leaning in. I choose to love her unconditionally, to trust her. We were similar in so many ways. We both had boxes in our basement rooted in sexual trauma, mistrust, abuse, abandonment, and a fear of never being enough. I had empathy and compassion for her traumatic experiences because that's all that little eighth-grade boy wanted to receive. That little boy once told himself that love alone is enough to endure any amount of pain and suffering and that being alone is the scariest thing ever. I feared abandonment and rejection so much that I tolerated mistrust and abuse and translated those behaviors into love and safety. After all, she loved me, didn't she?

While we were together—and even now that we were apart—our relationship brought to my attention the lingering pieces of trauma that were still within, pieces that I needed to explore further after hitting rock bottom again. But I believe in rock bottom. It's a place where I've learned I can rebuild an even stronger foundation of self-worth and self-love. At rock bottom, I can hear God screaming and encouraging me to get up. I think of that famous scene in *Rocky V* when Rocky says, "I didn't hear no bell"—that's the feeling of rock bottom. Everyone else sees you down, but you know deep inside the fight isn't over yet. It's the mantra from your inner warrior to get up off your knees, let your tears fall, find a shovel, and dig.

CHAPTER 15

Embrace the Heartbreak

Most of us never really learn how to embrace heartbreak. We don't know how to create healthy love stories of our own. We don't know that we are wearing rose-colored glasses until those red flags become landmines and scatter us to pieces. Perhaps that is because real heartbreak is the stuff they don't teach us in school or show us in most movies.

The closest we get to real heartbreak is watching *Sleepless in Seattle* or *The Notebook*. But real heartbreak goes beyond a Tom Hanks flick and never includes writing one love letter a day, every day for an entire year. Because if I did that, if I wrote the woman from Apartment 2 one letter a day, every day for a whole year, I'd probably be deemed a crazy person. But the truth is I wanted to do just that.

I would continue to struggle with accepting her need to let go. The last text message I would ever send would follow exactly four months after our breakup.

"Christine – you are the love of my life. And I genuinely don't know how to stop loving you. I don't know how to let that go. I don't know how to pretend or stop, as if what we shared didn't matter. My friend told me today, 'When you stop crying about those you lost, you stop caring.' I've been crying every single day. I miss you. All of you. And I wish you could trust that I do accept you. All

of you. I'm not afraid. I'm not scared. I accept whatever it is you need. And if you genuinely want me to leave you alone forever, as much as that hurts, I will still love you. If you stay away forever or decide to return, I'll always love you. I have no desire to seek anyone else. And never will. You have my heart, forever."

It was a message from my heart and one I felt called to share. I sent it sober, no drinks, no late-night 2 a.m. drunk-dialing. Just a note that expressed all my true feelings, and I meant every word. My soul begged to collide with hers. I wasn't sure I could ever find lightning in a bottle again. I wasn't sure I could ever feel what I felt for her with someone else. I loved her with all my being, so I accepted that I couldn't love anyone else.

In my attempt at closure, I stayed stuck, wanting to define and identify her avoidance, trauma, and reasoning for letting go—all of which created a tremendous amount of distraction for my own healing. Losing a soulmate plunged me into a tidal wave of emotions, a constant state of high tide that felt like drowning. Losing a soulmate brought an experience of high tide that caused me to drown in a sea of emotions. This loss felt worse than being alone in that hotel room in San Diego.

I stayed attached to something that had no movement. I was at a standstill. Yet, the nature of a wave is to have motion—to push forward and sometimes pull back. It has life. I had to embrace when the waves came rolling in and trust they would eventually move me to where I was meant to be, not where I wanted to be.

As summer drew near, it served as a constant reminder of everything I was missing out on. This summer was meant to include a family trip with her relatives, and I was doing my best to divert my thoughts from this reality. I pondered what her family might think of our split, reminiscing about the joyful times, our shared love for nature, and sunny days. We had plans to spend this summer together on Lake Michigan, but now, those plans were canceled. It was a new season, and Midwest summers, typically brimming with joy and excitement, now felt empty. I needed something that could distract me from those thoughts.

Perhaps I could fill the void with "stuff"—activities and adventures to keep me busy. I revisited my bucket list, considering dance classes, skydiving, and buying a motorcycle—a dream I'd had for years. It seemed like the perfect moment for an older Ducati, a modest yet thrilling purchase. Ducatis are to motorcycles what Ferraris are to cars: fast, exquisitely crafted, and sure to turn heads. In that moment, I couldn't imagine needing anything more than the Italian excellence of a Ducati in my life.

Riding that motorcycle demanded my undivided attention and precision, a stark contrast to driving my Jeep, where I could distract myself with music or podcasts. It was just me and my bike, embracing the open road. The mix of country roads and interstates made for an ever-changing landscape. On that bike, I discovered moments of joy, yet sadness would always loom close. One sweltering August morning, as I set out for my CrossFit class, I was about to learn just how vulnerable I was on those two wheels.

The sweltering summer sun beat down on my driveway as I felt the heat on my back, warming both my bike and me. I began to take off down my alleyway, slowly moving both feet onto the pegs. Once my feet came off the ground, I began to cry. *Not now*, I thought. How long would the grief last? My dark Ray Bans prevented anyone else from noticing, and because I was on my bike, I couldn't wipe my tears away, even if I wanted to. Instead, they fell as I slowly weaved in and out of the windy country road. In that moment, it hit me: I was alone.

I was no longer in my white Jeep heading to Apartment 2. I was on a motorcycle, heading to CrossFit class, but that wasn't where I wanted to be. I had to take that route at least four days a week, but it always triggered me. It meant having to take *her* exit to get to my class—the same exit I had taken for months, through snow-covered roads filled with joy, knowing I would be met with her sitting on her couch. The curse of being in a small Midwestern suburb, I suppose. I couldn't ignore that exit sign any more than I could ignore the unfolding lessons, both of which were painful.

Hugging a corner on a quiet country road, I began to question my relationship with God. *What was all this for?* I thought to myself as I drove past two cows grazing on the wet morning grass. I wanted to believe that if God loved me, he would have kept us together when I prayed for help before entering that dive bar. *If* he loved me, he could give me a sign that he was up there feeling my pain.

All I wanted was to be with the woman from Apartment 2, and we weren't together. I needed someone to blame other than myself, and I couldn't think of anyone better than the person who is supposed to "know it all." The same person who created all of us, according to my Christian understanding, and if he created me, then he knew this particular heartbreak was a part of my story.

My faith was quickly moving toward anger and resentment.

"What's your problem?" I shouted as I hugged the last bend of a coming straightaway.

"You have one job to do, and that's to love us unconditionally. To listen to us when we pray to you, when we need you the most! You're supposed to listen to us! You're supposed to heal the brokenhearted! Where are you?! WHY CAN'T YOU JUST DO YOUR DAMN JOB?!"

As soon as my last question fell from my mouth, my motorcycle stalled. Stuck at a red light on the way to I-65, my bike refused to start after three failed attempts, promptly shutting off each time it kicked over. The check engine light glaring back at me as tears of anger and sadness streamed down my face. I'm not a mechanic, but I knew that wasn't a good sign.. Removing my sunglasses and resting the kickstand, I sighed deeply and looked down, "What else do you want to take from me?" I mumbled to myself as I dismounted, oblivious to any potential oncoming traffic.

I pushed my bike onto the nearby sidewalk and called for a tow, feeling as though some higher power was insisting I pause my journey. It seemed ludicrous—blowing a Ducati's engine at a mere 25 miles per hour. I still wasn't sure what the purpose was in all of this, any of it. Yet, as I watched my bike being hoisted onto the tow truck, the sun glistening off the shiny chrome and mirrors, I realized my broken bike was a reflection of my own state. I had work to do, and I couldn't run from my work because I wanted to run toward the woman from Apartment 2. Instead, I had to run to me.

If I was ever going to fully heal, I had to unpack all my boxes again, one at a time. All those events that had left me broken needed to be looked at again. Maybe I could use them for good if I could only find a way to love myself a little more than I did before. Maybe Brandon's exercise of writing letters would serve a purpose again. I wasn't really sure where to even begin, but in that moment, I knew I needed to find a different kind of strength to face the pain that came with loss and this particular heartbreak. I had to embrace the heartbreak and loss because not everyone gets to experience it.

I needed to be open to the moments when Rick would attempt to challenge my thinking, even when those moments included questions I didn't want to answer or didn't like. No more hiding my stories—it was time to share everything with Rick, down to the details of what happened in eighth grade. My wounded inner child was the reason I risked continuing to repeat cycles that kept me holding onto partners, even when it was no longer safe to do so. He was voiceless and afraid. He was the most significant puzzle piece of my trauma and the root of all my fears.

My fears often held me back from experiencing a genuine love story, and if I continued to give in to those fears, it wouldn't just be my motorcycle that ended up broken—it would be me. Staying trapped in fear meant I was always living in the shadow of what was, unable to embrace what is. I had to come to terms with feeling completely shattered. My intense fear of abandonment and rejection led me to accept mistrust and abuse as forms of love and safety. I loved in this manner, believing that everyone deserves to experience love, thinking it could transform suffering into joy. However, the love I was giving wasn't healthy.

As my relationship with the woman from Apartment 2 began to reveal irreconcilable differences, I chose to overlook them, scared of our love story ending. I dismissed every warning sign, convinced she was my soulmate, believing love would see us through any challenge. I thought I was healed and ready to embrace our differences, but the truth is, there's no such state as being fully ready or completely healed. The loss of the woman from Apartment 2 served as a stark reminder that my journey of self-improvement is ongoing—that I'm not broken, just an endless work in progress.

I had to break away from being seduced by the thrill of chemistry and passion. Passion and chemistry are not the only tools needed for building and maintaining the type of relationship I seek. Passion flickers and fades in the storm. Passion is the drug that kept me holding onto a person who had already let go. Passion is what happens when I allow my heart to take over in place of my thoughts. I was addicted to the dopamine rush, and my body was beginning to detox as it separated from what was and slowly moved toward what is. Yes, I was struggling to detox, but I was beginning to heal, one day at a time.

*"Love and compassion are necessities, not luxuries.
Without them, humanity cannot survive."*

– Dalai Lama

CHAPTER 16

Forgiveness

I spent time— alone—in my favorite local coffee shop, reading self-help books while drinking the best London Fog ever. A typical coffee shop with local art on the walls and infectious energy made for an environment where reading and writing would become fun again. I had this silly vision that Christine would walk into that very same coffee shop one day. We would smile at each other in a way that acknowledges, *"I see you, and I love you,"* without needing to actually say anything. That it would be okay if we did.

Life will often show us what we need to repair within ourselves when a relationship ends; it certainly did for me. The hardest part of my healing journey was finding acceptance for the way my relationship ended. Rick would remind me that "not everyone who comes into my life is meant to stay." Some people stay just long enough to get attached to the feeling of two hearts beating under one set of sheets. Just long enough to remember how they take their coffee and the cute little dance they do in their kitchen while eating peanut butter out of the jar. Had I chosen to stay attached to the woman from Apartment 2, there would have been no movement, no growth.

I needed to heal from all the pieces of my story so they wouldn't end up in anyone's emotional backpack ever again. It wasn't their overhead baggage to claim; it was mine. I needed to tell Rick everything; I needed him to know all the boxes I kept in my basement. In my early sessions with Rick, he had taught me about "red flags," and this time, I needed to learn about love and how to let go. "Your willingness to suffer is real," Rick stated. "But I'm not sure how much benefit there is in unnecessary suffering. There is enough suffering in life, Paul. It is the unnecessary stuff, the stuff you can avoid, that you should avoid."

Rick was hitting me with brutal honesty, an honesty he often brought to our sessions, but this time, I was able to hear and receive the wisdom and relevancy of his words. Yes, the suffering was real; it was the last bit of connection I had to Christine, and I wanted to hold onto it. Holding on meant there was still hope. But Rick helped me understand that sometimes the things I most want to hold onto are also the things I most need to let go. There is both pain and purpose in letting someone go, and I was now beginning to understand what that purpose was.

Letting go creates a safe distance between my heart and my head. Letting go brings security and peace, acknowledging that everything in life is transient. Letting go leads to closure, even when I'm the only one who can grant it. If I hadn't let go, if I had clung to what was, I would eventually rot from the inside out, not the outside in. I would eventually lose everything on the outside as well. Rick was right—this was the unnecessary stuff.

Had I chosen to not let go, I would've stayed stuck chasing storm after storm until I eventually drowned. I would've lost all sense of self-worth and self-love. I would've lost my faith in God and my faith in ever finding love again. I would've allowed fear to win and love to lose. But I needed this experience. I needed to gain wisdom from this part of my story so I could learn when to let go. Most importantly, I had to turn inward all the love I wanted to give her and now give it to myself.

I gained compassion and a new perspective on loving differently, including self-compassion. She never had to love the way I loved, and I never had to love the way she loved. The essence of love isn't in mirroring each other's affection but in understanding and valuing our differences. It involves creating a safe space for expression and mutual understanding of each other's wants, needs and desires, and it has and holds boundaries. It's agreeing on the things that can cause harm to the very relationship you are building together. This time, I had to rebuild the relationship I had with myself; I had to find joy again.

I found that self-love embodies joy rather than happiness. To me, happiness is fleeting, like a checklist that eventually runs out. Happiness was the chase, like buying a motorcycle that broke down on the side of a road and never ran again. I had to shift from chasing temporary happiness to cultivating moments of joy—experiences that foster physical, spiritual, mental, and emotional growth. Healing from my past traumas, from feeling unseen and unheard, meant embracing progress as the path to a meaningful life filled with joy.

Moving forward meant embracing forgiveness, closure, and acceptance, enduring heartbreak to forge a stronger version of myself. I had to do this with Rick and by myself each morning before my kids woke up to meditate on loving what *is*, not what *was*. Loving what *is* created a consciousness of being in the moment rather than getting stuck in the past. Meditating in the quiet stillness of each morning reminded me why I deeply value connection and safety—the same things, I believe, that connect all of us.

I was reminded that it is possible to love someone new and that I can create new healthy relationships with myself and with others. I eventually downloaded those digital dating apps, not because I was ready, but because I needed to find joy in dating again. Joy in the journey and joy in meeting with a stranger. I wanted to see if I could use my list of boundaries to identify red flags this time around. But then I would delete them. I would often take one step forward and two steps back. I was still healing, and that's often what healing looks like—one step forward and two steps back.

I chose to embrace the heartbreak, just like my friend Josh encouraged me to do. I chose to find confidence in being a stranger in a coffee shop or a dive bar as my friend Dave sings karaoke to a crowd of three. I chose to let my tears fall and embrace the sea of emotions when they come rushing in because high tide will always remind me of the loss of a love story, not a life story. I chose to bravely share all my pieces, even the ones that are torn and tattered with jagged edges, just like an old hoodie with studs and safety pins. Because, after all, those torn and tattered pieces are often the most authentic and the most beautiful.

CHAPTER 17

Don't Stop Believing

As summer came to a close, I couldn't have asked for a better place to be. I had family, friends, and the love of my two boys. I spent more time with them and embraced the constant joy and love they have for the little things because the joy of a child is hard to miss. We would chase fireflies, build bigger forts, and discover new adventures together. When my youngest would ask to play, it wasn't always easy to say yes, but I did it anyway because I wanted to keep moving forward. I wanted to find a way to bring joy to the ending of a summer that almost broke me.

I decided I didn't need another motorcycle, but I did want a new adventure. An adventure that was just for me, one that I didn't have to share with anyone. I signed up for dance lessons, a talent I never had. It wasn't anything like a Ducati, but I figured learning to dance could be an exciting challenge. My instructor, full of radiance and joy, met me each week on her dance floor, ready to guide a complete beginner like me. I needed the richness of moments like that. Moments where I could authentically show up in a vulnerable way to learn something I would have never considered had I not experienced this particular heartbreak.

Dancing, I realized, mirrored love in many ways. It demanded intimacy and connection. Learning to dance meant mastering a few basic steps and patterns, unlike the patterns I had repeated in my relationships. These dance patterns were designed for joy and with purpose. Regardless of the music, it was about partnership—one leading and the other following. Dancing led me to a fresh perspective on self-love, teaching me to express myself through movement. Just as Brandon once guided me to embrace my inner warrior, this period of heartbreak showed me how to shed my armor and learn the two-step.

During my Hero's Journey with Brandon, he encouraged me to write letters of forgiveness—both to those I sought forgiveness from and those I wished to forgive, including a letter to myself. "What does Paul need to forgive Paul for?" he would ask. This question often echoed in my mind. Brandon emphasized that these letters weren't meant for anyone else but me, underscoring that forgiveness begins with oneself. This process was crucial for my journey towards self-worth and self-love.

After writing these letters, I followed his advice to read them aloud to myself, standing in front of my bedroom mirror so that I was the sole audience. Each letter peeled away layers of understanding. Although the thought of never sharing these letters pained me, Brandon's wisdom rang true. The affirmations on my bathroom mirror, like the words in those letters, were messages intended solely for me. When I finally got to the letter I had addressed to myself, I read it aloud and paused before finishing the last few words:

> *"I forgive you, I love you, you are enough,*
> *you aren't broken, and you are worthy.*
> – Love, Paul."

As I finished reading that last letter, I paused for a moment. I remembered those words I wrote on my bathroom mirror: I am worthy, I am love, I am ready. I remembered that my past is not my present; I can change my story at any time. Most of all, forgiveness is a journey that is never easy and often brings tremendous pain and loss. I was reminded that pain and heartbreak can bring with them incredible lessons if I choose to dig. That the process of forgiveness is constant, and that pain is a reminder that we are still here - that life is never a straight line. I remembered that warriors don't wipe their tears; they let them fall. Most importantly, I remembered that I am not broken—none of us are.

Epilogue

Part of my healing process included a lot of journaling. On August 5th, 2021, I wrote the following entry:

"Dear Paul,

Many of us go through massive loss and pain on our journey of love, and I want you to put this journal down for a moment and out loud remind yourself that you are enough, just as you are. You are not broken. You are enough, just as you are. Highlight that sentence. Read it again and again until it resonates in your very being.

You are not broken. You are enough, just as you are.

You are beautiful, strong, and worthy. You are created for a purpose and with purpose. You are not a mistake of your past. You do not have to stay attached to someone who doesn't see your worth or stay stuck replaying your trauma in unhealthy, lopsided relationships. You can change the headline of your story the moment you seek to move beyond what was and step forward into what is. You are not broken pieces but beautiful pieces. Pieces that may be torn and tattered but remain the very pieces that make up the beautiful person you are today."

That entry is one that I often go back to when I feel like I'm broken. It's a reminder that the heartbreak may be real; it may even bring me to my knees, but I'm still here. My story isn't over yet. There's still plenty of ink in my pen, and I can still write a new chapter. I didn't have to erase what was in order to step toward a new future. Instead, I needed to stretch and grow into someone bigger. I needed to grow beyond the pain to make room for new love.

I learned I wasn't alone either. Heartbreak is pretty universal. It's something we all experience if we are brave enough to open up and let someone in. Hurt people tend to hurt other people. But changed people often change people. I was still hungry for change and growth, and I was still meeting with Rick by phone every week because there will always be a need for me to share with someone like him. Someone who can champion my story and keep me grounded and focused on my self-worth and self-love. Someone who can equip me with the tools necessary so that I no longer experience unnecessary suffering.

I believe we all need someone like Rick, someone who can create space for us to share as we unpack our boxes filled with stories, trauma, triggers, and heartbreak because we all have stuff we haven't let go of yet. Stuff that, for a moment, can make us feel like we are broken when really we are all capable of healing and worthy of love if we can honestly face ourselves. Stuff that, for a moment, can keep us small as we continue to take steps toward healing. I was able to find healing because I was telling my story, all of it. And not just to Rick, but to anyone willing to listen.

We all have trauma, triggers, and childhood wounds, so when we tell someone we love them, we must also be ready to love those pieces. What we have gone through often informs us of how we choose to look at the world around us. Our experiences shape our worldview, and the scars from our past traumas are often the root of our present triggers. Reacting to these triggers might push away the very person ready to support us through our healing process. Without confronting our past, we risk repeating the same patterns. The richness of intimacy requires a willingness to be brave and authentic, and that authenticity and bravery always start with loving ourselves first.

Healing is a journey we don't have to embark on alone, though we're ultimately responsible for our own recovery. Failing to address our issues can leave us anchored in the past. I had to stop bringing my past into my present. This experience instilled a belief that I am capable of healing and that I can choose to love again, no matter the heartbreak. That I am worthy of a real love story. I choose to stay true to my boundaries and deal-breakers while being open to new experiences. Most importantly, I will not sacrifice my self-worth or self-love on the altar of unhealthy love ever again.

As I began to share my story with Rick and my friends, I learned that there are many people out there just like me. Individuals who have held onto boxes that they, too, have struggled to share. I am grateful for those experiences, because they have brought depth to our connection and a bond that no one can ever take away. If we don't share with each other, we will never go deep enough to accept the person we've become. We will never fully see ourselves or anyone else if we choose to withhold. If we don't accept who we are, we may never accept anyone else. We may run from love because it's "yucky and gross." So, find the courage to love yourself.

I believe in the power of storytelling, and I want you to know that you are not alone as you embark on your journey of self-worth and self-love. It takes courage to share your boxes, so start small if you must. Unpack them one at a time. Find the courage to share where you are on your path of healing whenever you are ready to, just as I choose to share my story with you. You may find greater peace and greater healing by sharing your story, just as I have. Most importantly, when you are ready to share, I trust you will find other people out there just like you, people who are trying to do all they can to be seen and loved. And always remember, you are not broken; you are enough, and you deserve to be loved.

THANK YOU FOR READING MY BOOK!

Scan the QR Code to learn more about the author.

I appreciate your interest in my book and value your feedback as it helps me improve future versions of this book. I would appreciate it if you could leave your invaluable review on Amazon.com with your feedback. Thank you!

"If you let go a little, you will have a little peace. If you let go a lot, you will have a lot of peace. If you let go completely, you will have complete peace."

– Ajahn Chah

Acknowledgments

Writing this book would have never been possible if it weren't for the beautiful lessons learned and the love shared with the woman from Apartment 2. I'm sorry for any unnecessary hurt and pain I may have caused. I genuinely hope you are experiencing a world of joy, one with an abundance of self-love. I forever believe that you will write the most extraordinary love story ever.

Thank you, Bob Goff, for our four-minute phone call on November 2nd, 2020, when you encouraged me that anyone can write a book and that every book starts with one word. I would often reflect on that phone call when I felt stuck and was reminded of the generosity and wisdom you shared that day. Your gift and talents in writing are rooted in faith and love, and are truly unmatched. I look forward to remaining a lifelong fan and reading all your future work.

Special thanks to Adrian Gostick for believing in this book and providing me with resources and support before I even drafted a sentence. Both you and Chester Elton remain near and dear. I'm so grateful for your friendship and infectious enthusiasm in promoting a world that always looks to seek joy and gratitude.

*NOTE: Adrian and Chester run a podcast called **Anxiety at Work**, and they continue to be leaders in the business world, promoting and cultivating a strong culture.*

To my editor, Rachel Rueckert, I am so grateful for your talent in developmental and copy editing. You instilled a belief and encouragement that helped each chapter find life and more significant meaning. Rachel is a profound author, having recently published her second book, *If The Tide Turns*.

Special thanks to Rick for the many years of counseling. You're a light in every storm that has attempted to consume my very being and a steadying influence in every high tide. I love you.

To my pastor and church, for providing a place of worship when all hope felt lost, and the reminder that God does answer prayers if I choose to seek Him first. Thank you for providing us shelter in the storm, which can often bring together a beautiful group of people seeking a spiritual connection and place of worship.

Thank you, Rob C., for reading my book and for encouraging me as a writer. I will forever cherish our late-night phone calls, bourbons floating in your pool, and the love you and your wife choose to give to me. I'm looking forward to visiting soon.

Thank you, Gregg, for the decade you've spent pouring into me. Your generosity and guidance have helped to mold and shape me in ways I've never imagined. I deeply cherish our friendship. I aspire to be like you when I grow up.

A very special thanks to John Kim. You have forever changed the landscape for what self-help and healing looks like in a modern digital world. You have influenced me more than you know.

To Wrabel, thank you for writing "Poetry," a song that will forever remind me of the first September I met the woman from Apartment 2.

To NF, please continue to be brave and authentic. Your lyrics hold such a special place in my life and my heart. Thank you for understanding how difficult this thing called life is and for staying rooted in faith, even when life doesn't make any sense.

Josh, you came back into my life at my most significant time of need. Your note to *"embrace the heartbreak"* was such an influential piece of this writing. You're an amazing father and friend. Remember, the light you seek is already within.

My heartfelt thanks to Michael Hageman for your friendship and unwavering support from the very beginning of my writing journey. Your invitation to be a guest on your podcast and your continued encouragement have meant the world to me.

Stephan Jenkins, thank you for continuing to write songs that speak to my soul. Your artistry and lyricism paint a vivid story in authenticity and raw emotion. Thank you for being brave enough to share your pain with us. You are an extraordinary storyteller.

Monica, you made learning fun and inclusive, encouraging us to share our thoughts and dive deep into literature. Your classes were a joy, filled with engaging discussions and a safe space to explore ideas. Years later, I leaned on you for feedback on my book, and you made me feel valued once again. Thank you for everything.

A special thank you to the Millers, who dragged me out of my home and generously fed me plenty of Totino's™, bourbon, and love at a time when I thought I had lost everything. For all the tears, playlists, laughter, and card games—all moments I will forever remember—thank you.

Brandon, words can't even begin to describe the gratitude I feel for having stumbled across you. Thank you for teaching me what it takes to become a warrior. You are a tremendous gift that this Universe gets to experience, and I'm so grateful I got to share in your wisdom at a time when I lost a big part of me. (Brandon co-hosts a podcast entitled *Mankind Project,* which empowers men to take off their masks and tackle their tough stuff!)

Jack, you have been a beacon of light and guidance for over a decade. I am so honored and grateful to learn from you. Our trip to Sedona is one I will deeply cherish. Thank you for always creating space for me to be seen and heard, for challenging me in a gentle way, and for your compassion, grace, and stewardship. Many of my lessons shared in this book are from your teachings. My greatest wish is to provide a ripple of healing and to share the wisdom you hold with the world.

Sabrina, you are such a remarkable friend. I'm beyond grateful for the decade-plus spent sharing, learning, and growing from your faith-driven wisdom. No matter how difficult it was to hear or read your beautiful words, they continued to push me closer to God, healing, and acceptance. Thank you for always being there through all the late-night calls.

Grandma, thank you for always allowing me to explore creative outlets. For buying me books, submitting my artwork to your employer, and for purchasing my first set of CDs so that I could experience The Beatles and Green Day for the first time. I will forever cherish that time when we used to send notes to each other in our own secret code. Your wit, joy, and heart for others are unmatched. I am so grateful to be your grandson.

Rachel, thank you for being my biggest supporter and unwavering champion. Your love for me and my boys, and your constant encouragement to fervently pursue God, mean everything to me. I am profoundly grateful that God brought us together, and I eagerly look forward to building a life that overflows with His joy, servitude, and adventure. Let's always keep Him first.

Dominic and Dakota, I hope you two grow up to be brave and authentic. Seek joy and continue to serve and love others. Stay God-centered in all the relationships that you build. Most importantly, remember to seek Him in all you do. That is where you will find self-love and self-worth no matter what storms come your way.

To all my friends and family who have stood by me through every season of life, through the heartbreak and the joy, for all the late-night phone calls and space created, you are my foundation when I waver. Thank you for always standing with me. I love each of you deeply.

Lastly, thank you, dear reader, for taking the time to read my story. I genuinely hope, wherever you are, that you can love yourself. Find the courage to share, to grow, to accept, and forgive. Most importantly, if you struggle to let go, know that you are not alone. Sometimes we don't have to let go of someone to find love again. We just have to remember to love ourselves a little bit more.

www.ingramcontent.com/pod-product-compliance
Lightning Source LLC
Chambersburg PA
CBHW070332090426
42733CB00012B/2458